Acknowledgments

I WISH TO THANK a few people for helping me be here with something real and useful to offer.

First, I offer my deepest appreciation to my heart teacher Dabsang Rinpoche, who showed me that there was no box unless I wanted one. Even after his passing he has continued to love and assist me in the most tangible and unimaginable ways. To Glen Gerhardt, my high school creative writing teacher, who helped me to get the frequency of writing—although he would never have thought to call it that. I thank Michael Broffman for opening my windows to Chinese medicine, and also because he was the one who, in December 1979, first took my pulse and described my life in a way that I could understand. The work I have been so fortunate to do is directly related to his influence. I thank Karen Joiner for healing beyond my wildest imagination. To my wonderful son Namkai Michael Fairfield, who has taught me more than I will ever teach him. And to Conde Freeman Fairfield, who loves and supports in a way I had never thought possible, and who has shown me the reality of Deep Happy.

Last but not least, I must thank Jan Johnson of Red Wheel/Weiser, who recognized something and coerced me with love and creative allowances and then bounced it and wacked it in such a pleasant way that I enjoyed finishing a book that has been working its way out of me for a long time.

Names and in some cases identifying personal details have been changed, but all of the stories are true and represent experiences that are not only possible, but likely if we just open to the possibility of them.

This book is dedicated to the benefit of all beings.

Contents

Praise for *Deep Happy*

"Many words have been written about happiness, that elusive state of mind and body that most people desire but often find beyond their grasp. Dr. Peter Fairfield presents a unique approach that delves into those blocks to happiness that keep too many people from appreciating the pleasure and fulfillment that each moment of their lives has to offer. He presents activities and humor along with insights from meditation, the martial arts, Chinese medicine, and quantum physics. After I finished reading this splendid book I felt happier and I think that most of his readers will have a similar experience."

—Stanley Krippner, PhD, professor of Psychology, Saybrook University, co-author, *Personal Mythology*

"Written by an author who has over forty years in the healing profession, *Deep Happy* explores the journey towards spiritual peace and inner contentment. Peter Fairfield offers his extensive experience, study of many ancient philosophies and his intuitive knowing, to show that true happiness comes from a deepening connection to our own inner being. *Deep Happy* is filled with many helpful practices and the author's personal experiences encouraging the reader to relinquish redundant beliefs and find true happiness."

—Christine Page, MD, speaker and author of *Frontiers of Health*

"Through the years, Peter Fairfield has found the secret of happiness for his own life and has shared it with thousands of people. Now he brings it to us in this delightful book so we can find our own inner peace and happiness."

—Gladys T. McGarey, MD, MD[H]

"*Deep Happy* takes us to the place within each of us that is already happy and connected. Fairfield describes a journey that can be easy, fascinating, and even inspiring."

—Ken Dychtwald, PhD, author of *A New Purpose: Redefining Money, Family, Work, Retirement, and Success* and *Gideon's Dream: A Tale of New Beginnings*

"For people reaching out for deeper levels of happiness, here is an inspired tutorial offering a surprising and practical path. The wit and wisdom of *Deep Happy* is arrayed in 15 enlightening chapters that can easily become a two-week adventure of self-transformation where you wake up each day entertaining different ideas about yourself and practicing new habits—all under the rare genius of a gentle giant named Peter. How lucky they are who find this book!"

—David B. Chamberlain, PhD, DHL, Psychologist, and author of the international best seller, *The Mind of Your Newborn Baby*

"In today's world there is so much that disempowers us; we forget we have the capacity to make a real difference by bringing joy to others and to all that we do. For this reason, finding a book that affirms us as joyful, creative, empowered persons can be life-changing. *Deep Happy* offers all these things and more, a road map to be all that we can be."

—David Spangler, author of *The Laws of Manifestation* and *Apprenticed to Spirit*

Introduction

THIS BOOK IS NOT about happiness—it is about Deep Happy. It is not really about positive thinking, getting what we want, or abundance, though with Deep Happy you will access all of these and, more importantly, the places where you resist them. Deep Happy is about dropping beneath the fray to a place within each of us that is already very much alive and well. Deep Happy is nothing we have to buy or get. We already have it! We just have to remember where it is, make friends with it, and invite it out to play.

Our "quick-fix" culture is used to popping a pill or an attitude against anything that is at all uncomfortable. We are unaccustomed to finding comfort in the parts of us that we have learned to push away, usually since our days in the womb. Culturally, we are an iconic mélange of neon and free offers pulling us every which way except for the way home—to ourselves.

We have reduced our understanding of enlightenment to something that describes perfume and political commentary, missing the deeper transcendent meaning: the union with and the acceptance of all that is—first the light *and the dark* and then the infinite held in simple awareness.

In my sixty-plus years of trying to understand myself and other people, I have found that we all mostly want the same things, though the words might be different for each of us. We want to feel safe; we want an easy connection to life; we want vitality, energy, a healthy body and something meaningful and interesting to do with our time. The process of Deep Happy connects us to all of that, because these things are intrinsic to each of us and are in fact necessary for our fulfillment as evolving beings.

Vitality comes as we free the physical body, first from our patterns of trauma and emotional hurt, and then from the limits we have imposed on our senses of feeling and pleasure. *Energy* comes as we free our emotional and energetic hearts, allowing and opening our interactions with life in all its myriad forms. *Intelligence* and real wisdom come as the coherence of our bodies and hearts create a healed foundation for seeing things as they really are, from the finite to the infinite. And finally, real safety comes as we directly experience our timeless essence, untouched by the vagaries of life, death, and the calamities in between. This is the path of Deep Happy.

1

Beginning Deep Happy

When a fool hears the Tao, he laughs . . . the utter simplicity!

—Dao De Jing

Happiness is your nature, It is not wrong to desire it
What's wrong is seeking it outside,
When it is inside.

—Ramana Marharshi

JUST LIKE THE GREAT seas and oceans that are unaffected by huge and raging storms on the surface just a few feet above, we can experience the ebb and flow of conflicting and difficult events of the world outside of us, yet still connect to the stillness, peace, and happiness in the deep and essential parts of us. In other words, once you get used to it, you can exist in the crazy world and still remain calm, connected, and aware inside. This is the essential message of Deep Happy.

Everyone wants to be happy. It's what drives the good and the craziness of the world. The quest for happiness is the basis in some way for everything we do. All forms of life want to be happy, even the tiniest of us. I remember in high school looking at amoebas under a microscope. I put a very tiny particle of meat on the slide. All the amoebas rushed to get to it, like a big pre-holiday sale at Macy's. It was very clear that the particular amoeba that got the protein experienced something quite different than the other amoebas. The one who got it seemed happy, if you can say that about an amoeba. Its body expanded, while the others seemed frustrated, their little bodies contracting and bumping into each other as they moved away. Their patterns and movements were very different than they were before they went after and lost the food. All forms of life, even microscopic organisms, experience transient happiness—if not on the emotional level, then at least on the chemical, neuronal, and survival level. As potentially conscious beings, we have the opportunity to experience the place inside of us that is safe and connected: that is Deep Happy.

It might seem easy to be happy, but happiness can be elusive and paradoxical. Reading, driving a car, and even walking seem easy, but we had to learn how to do them by letting their processes become imprinted into our nervous systems and daily patterns. If we want to excel, we can take advanced training to read faster, drive better, and walk and exercise more efficiently. Learning to experience Deep Happy is very similar.

You might be wondering, "Why do I need to learn to be happy? Shouldn't I just fix my problems? Wouldn't that make me happy?" That's a fair question, but you are reading this book, I assume, for a reason. Either you haven't been able to fix your problems or think you have already done so and you still feel like something is missing.

The odd thing is, it often happens that at just the moment when we finally feel happy—when we get our new car, find the tax documents we have been looking for all day, or even just get a moment of peace—something else comes up and takes a bite out of our happiness. This kind of happiness, although certainly welcome whenever it comes, is transient. It is a kind of happiness that depends on something happening or not happening. It is not a happiness that we can count on; most of the time, we can't even predict what will bring it or how long it will last.

So let's re-examine what happiness really is. On a superficial level we can say it is a generalized experience of feeling and sensations caused by many things that we usually lump together: satisfaction, resolution, safety, and reward. We eat a good meal when we are hungry; buy a new espresso maker when our old one breaks; feel the morning sun after a cold night; appreciate a good listener; win an argument; fall in love; end a bad relationship; start and finish a great book. This list could go on to fill a whole library. All of these things and probably most that you can imagine involve some kind of change—some thing or situation becoming better.

Much of our time involves seeking or refuting something to attain happiness. This is a never-ending process. As we grow and develop, it becomes more and more subtle. For instance, feeling good about ourselves because we didn't want or need something seems more developed than succumbing to the desire, but it is still part of the process of cause and effect. We remain in this mode until we come upon another way. For most of us, ending the cycle of "searching and getting" usually means we have left our bodies.

The deeper happiness inside of us is a happiness that does not change. It has a different quality than the outer experiences of satisfaction and safety. It is like a wonderful tone that vibrates subtly and pervasively throughout our bodies and within each cell, thought, and perception. As outer challenges and problems absorb our attention, a part of us always remains unchanged. Our core essence is always in resonance with a deep and profound happiness. We just have to remember that it is there waiting for us.

Most of us have had at least some happiness in our lives. For many people these momentary peaks of happiness are what hold us together through the tedium and routine of everyday life. But I ask you: What happens to the experience of being happy all the rest of the time? It may surprise you to know that many of us resist deeper happiness without knowing it. We get very used to being and staying just the way we are, often with great limits to our ability to feel pleasure, ease, joy, and especially personal satisfaction and even simple fun. These limitations are learned restrictions that either match with the patterns and tone of our birth families or are the result of overwhelming physical or emotional trauma, which then anchor themselves in the structures of our physical and energetic body. These blockages can stay with us until we find a way to heal and release them. As you read this book, you will be able to uncover and heal these blockages.

Deep Happy Inner Practice

Take a few moments to relax and close your eyes. Breathe into your lower abdomen and feel your breath move in and out. Let yourself relax into your body. Listen to and feel your breath expanding and relaxing in your lower tummy.

Let yourself remember feeling happy. Let the memory of that feeling awaken in your body. Can you let your body feel happy? Notice if there are any parts of your body that feel less happy than other parts, or that don't feel anything at all. Your pelvis, neck, shoulders, and chest are common areas of emotional holding. Try to let the physical feeling of happiness gently flow into these uncharted waters. See if over time you can let every cell in your body vibrate with the tone of deep connectedness and Deep Happy.

Think about things that make you happy. When that seems clear, remember times when you felt deeply happy.

Remember how your body felt during these times. If that is not easy for you to do, feel your breath in your lower abdomen again while at the same time remembering your happy moments. Happiness is first and foremost a body experience.

To get to Deep Happy we first have to reacquaint our bodies with the physical experience of pleasant sensations, then physical happiness. No hurry—just let yourself get used to it over time.

We grew up believing that certain basic attitudes and ways of being create inner happiness: kindness, stillness, generosity, forgiveness, and being in the *now.* We are encouraged to be peaceful, still, and calm. However, when we do drop into that moment of quiet and clarity, what often arises is everything inside us that is not quiet and not clear: our worries, fears, memories, feelings, withheld expressions, and doubts. These inner voices can have a wide polarity. Part of Deep Happy is learning what to do when we notice this happening. On the good side, they can range from easy thoughts that creatively inform and remind us of things we need to notice, remember, or think about. But they can also manifest as physical and emotional numbness or raging storms of confusion and intense feelings that can overtake us, eventually filling all available space with inner noise and powerful diverting images. Most of us live somewhere in between, though the voices of guidance and wisdom are always there—even when they are hard to hear.

We learn from our families and society to "protect" ourselves with these internal thoughts and voices so that we stay away from the feelings and emotions that are locked away deep in our bodies. To do this we either make ourselves numb or we use the excessive stimulation of all the "things" of the world. Though we unconsciously put them there to protect us, in reality they keep us from ourselves. This is the great confusion of our current world. The setup is this:

We have our natural inner clarity and guidance. It gets covered up by confused thoughts, conflicting emotions, and uncomfortable physical sensations. On top of that we surround ourselves with the frenzy of our busy lives or the dullness of being stuck without knowing what we really want. When we can begin to turn our attention back in and finally notice the comfortable place inside of us, we can release the "goop" and find our way to a life that gets easier—much easier.

Our world supports the drama of our continuing misery with all the diversions we could ever need, all the enabling mythology and for many of us a political, economic and social milieu that holds us in a perpetual state of unease and concern and clouds over the many positive things that are also occurring. Many of us are able to deal with the intensity of modern life by finding some quiet time now and then. This is a good thing—it is the only way that we can calm our overtaxed nervous systems. But sometimes the apparent experience of stillness and inner reflection can in reality be dullness, numbness, and disconnection masquerading as peace and calm. Closing off from the craziness of the world is a healthy tack in the short term. But to emerge from the craziness whole and clear with our wits about us takes a different strategy. We may not initially be able to remove ourselves from our daily challenges, but we can learn to listen to ourselves again, even in the midst of the fray, and in so doing, reawaken the real peaceful and happy place that is always within us. With a little practice, this sacred place can be a reliable source we can find our way back to again and again, until we finally get it that we never have to leave.

To accomplish this we must begin by discovering who we really are and living in the world as it really is. The merging of these creates a synergy that is both pragmatic and creative; it eliminates the effects of most of the things that trouble us.

One of the important stages in developing this personal coherence comes as we unite the voices inside of us. We have all experienced "I should, I shouldn't" conversations with ourselves. We have all done or said one thing while thinking or feeling something quite different. These mixed voices can counterbalance the effect of our initial good actions and overshadow or shift the wisdom, energy, and tone of our original good idea. These shifts in outcome can also come from trying to do the "right thing" or listening to our head without taking the time to sense the deeper wisdom of what our heart is telling us. A famous story from Nepal illustrates this very well.

In the 1970s, a U.S. Peace Corps worker in Nepal decided that the several-thousand-year-old tradition of terracing the hillside rice fields so that they slanted downward could be improved upon. He figured that slanting the fields inward toward the hills could conserve water. His Peace Corps team spent a huge amount of time and energy restructuring all the ancient rice fields, encouraging the local villagers to restructure their way of doing things that had worked for thousands of years. It seemed to work at first, but as the first rainy season wore on, the water that had pooled up in the area where the field met the hill began to seep underground. Eventually the ground underneath the fields eroded. All the rich earth that had been developed for centuries slid down the hill, ruining the local economy and leaving many previously prosperous villages without food or livelihood.

Obviously, the Peace Corps worker had a good intent. But his desire to "do good" and his lack of appreciation for the knowledge and practical experience of the Nepalese farmers kept him from seeing that he was making a bad decision. These patterns of personality that cause us to act and react are often very hard for us to see in ourselves. They have probably been with us since the womb, and are what hold us so firmly because we are so used to them. They are primarily patterns in the body and nervous system, but they are also the accumulation of certain conceptual ideas that we hold as sacrosanct. We call the accumulation of these influences our outer personality. The good news is that we can change.

I do much of my work over the phone with people from all over the world. I was working with a physician and acupuncturist in Chicago who was questioning why her practice was not growing as she wanted it to. I had her take a moment and imagine her practice becoming very busy, with many new and interesting clients. As she did this, her voice tightened a little and I could tell that a part of her was resisting the idea. As with many of us, her head wanted one thing, but the rest of her perceived the idea of more clients and greater success in a different way.

My client's professional training had taught her that to be a good physician one has to be very serious and professional. She did not allow flowing energy and physical renewal to be part of her personal experience while performing her clinical duties. The more clients she worked with, the more worn out and resistant she became.

My client had not learned to nourish herself while working. She expended energy, but she was not used to taking it in at the same time. She failed to create a reciprocal loop—A process of putting out energy through action and intent and simultaneously allowing energy to flow back. Again, this is a common cause of burnout and work dissatisfaction.

I worked to help her shift both her energetic patterns and her learned concepts about what success looks like. I showed her how to reprogram her physical patterns of subtly tightening various parts of her body, so that by the end of the session when she pictured herself with more clients, her physical and energetic body opened and she felt a deep ease and happiness. Pretty much everyone has patterns like my client's, and they are easy to change. It just takes a little bit of time, study, openness, and honest curiosity.

Deep Happy Inner Practice

Think back to a situation when you went against what your inner voice was telling you.

Perhaps afterward, it was obvious that things might have turned out differently if you had trusted what you knew to be true. This gap between our wisdom and our actions is the focus of this practice.

Start by just beginning to notice what you really feel or think about things and events going on around you. Pick an area that is not going as you would like it to.

Pay attention to your secondary thoughts and feelings. If you are trying to do something, notice if there are any other voices or opinions in your head. At first just notice and listen. When you have an extra moment, see if you can complete each of the other thoughts: "This is not a good idea because . . ." or "I don't deserve this because . . ." and so forth. You might be surprised at what comes out. Also notice the sound and tone of each of your dissenting voices. They often sound remarkably similar to one of our inner parents or the voice of our parents.

One of the basic truths that Buddha taught is that "life is suffering." This might sound a little pessimistic for a cool guy like the Buddha. But what I think he meant was that life is suffering only if we live and find our meaning in the outer world of cause and effect, ebb and flow—a life where we only pay attention to material things and don't discover the deeper unchanging reality that dissolves suffering. This inner connection is the source of the solutions that our world so desperately needs.

Buddha taught that all suffering comes from only three sources: desire, aversion, and ignorance. In other words, wanting something we don't have; not wanting something we already have or are afraid we will get; or misperceiving or ignoring what is right in front of us. In other words, suffering is caused by feeling that we cannot be happy unless the reality around us meets our expectations.

Here is something to think about:

All of the things you can think of that make you happy are relative! All of the things that *make* us happy tend to change. When they change, so can the possibility of our happiness.

Deep Happy is just what is left when everything else disappears.

Most of us live in what my wife Conde calls a "Hamster Nation"—we endlessly run through our lives, rarely getting off the wheel of outer experience and activity to touch the intrinsic deeper reality. We are often so busy or "tuned out" that we miss the full experience of living in our miraculous physical body that anchors us to our multifaceted world and to the experience of simply being.

For some, this endless "Hamster Nation" activity can even involve sitting on the couch, closing off from the activities of outer life through dullness and habit. Please don't get me wrong here. We all have a right to sit on the couch and veg out. I personally love my couch. It is a joy to come home and find my safe place to sit, away from the intensity or boredom of life, and feel like things are okay again, at least for a little while.

A few years ago, after an agonizing divorce, I rented a house on a mountain by the sea just north of San Francisco. I spent my first month there sitting on my couch, staring out at the changing colors of the vast ocean, not even thinking, just being. It was all I could do. This was a conscious choice and a strategy for beginning the process of healing and discovering where to take my life next. But if sitting on the couch (or wherever our "soft place" is) is all that we do every night—pushing the world away rather than to creatively and consciously opening up to it—then we are still running on that hamster wheel. Of course, it can be a very good thing to "find our cave" and hang out there until the storm passes, but when the storm is over we get to go outside again. It can also be an interesting process to bundle up and go for a walk in the storm, enjoying the power and beauty of it.

We all have a right to our own version of the hamster wheel. However, it will not bring us lasting fulfillment or Deep Happy until we begin to accept ourselves as we are and open our senses to the events that engulf us. As we begin to accept, we find a level of living that is not dependent on the transient events of the world. Before long, the fleeting interest and excitement of the good meal or new shoes will, rather than wearing off, connect us via these wonderful sensory experiences to the intrinsic biological happiness that is within each of us. This is when our constant search for the "unknown something" begins to quiet and our hamster wheel begins to slow down. Please don't misunderstand me. I love the outer things of the world: shopping, travel, sex, food, even football. But the deepest part of my experience does not depend on any of those things.

Most of us are in the habit of limiting the amount of joy or even basic nourishment and happiness that we can let in. Just the other day I was working with a patient, Ellen, who was not able to hear anything good about herself. She would not accept anything that I said to her that was positive.

"You must have a lot of inner strength to handle the death of your husband the way you did," I said to her.

"Uh-huh," she mumbled, staring out the window.

"You really are survivor."

"Oh yes, I am that," she answered, responding to the memory of the pain, rather than the accomplishment of keeping it together through her difficult time, which was what I was trying to encourage her with.

How many times have we taken in criticism, detail by judgmental detail, feeling the sharp sting of someone's recrimination, yet letting kind, loving, and encouraging words fly right by us without the slightest notion that they might actually be true? This is a mild form of post-traumatic stress, though for some of us some it is not so mild. Our bodies and nervous systems learn to minimize stimulus to avoid any kind of overwhelm.

The great quandary of modern life is that it teaches us to minimize or deny deeper happiness and pleasure, while at the same time compelling us to seek it out.

While I was writing this book, I got a call from a woman named Melissa. She was reorganizing her life after separating from her husband upon finding out that he and her best friend had been having an affair for over a year. Her previous life training had taught her to push her feelings and body sensations away. In our phone session, we worked to have her begin to feel the intense feelings of anger and betrayal that she had kept at bay by keeping parts of her body numb. She told me that she initially felt very uncomfortable as the previously denied feelings came up, but as they passed she began to feel coherent in a way that was new to her and let her feel stronger and more hopeful than she had in many years.

The great quandary of modern life is that it teaches us to minimize or deny deeper happiness and pleasure, while at the same time compelling us to seek it out.

I often use the analogy of a dry sponge in my classes and seminars. Dry sponges do not easily absorb moisture. It takes them a little time to get used to the water; then they gradually begin to take it in. Many of us are like that. We have our set points for nourishment, love, attention, and intimacy. Whenever our comfortable limit is breached, our physical and emotional defenses begin to tighten up.

My family had almost no physical closeness. In my early twenties I lived in a spiritual community where everyone did a lot of hugging. For the first six months, when someone hugged me, I felt stiff and uncomfortable. Hugging made me nervous because I was not used to it. In time I learned to like it. For many of us, love, caring, self-acceptance, and nurturing take getting used to. The practice of opening our selves involves first noticing our discomfort, then watching it, and gradually, as we are ready, relaxing into whatever the fuller experience is.

We all have likes and dislikes, but if they become too important, they get in our way. The soup is too salty, my knee is painful, I do not have enough time to get everything done, my co-worker will not stop talking about herself, and so forth. It is not that there isn't some validity to each of these, but if we get too invested in any of them, our energy and balance get sucked away and our fuse gets shorter. Each of these situations involves something that requires change. It is certainly no problem to either change or not eat the soup or to have a conversation with our fellow employee. But what if it is something we cannot change? What if our painful knee or our schedule cannot be improved? This is where Deep Happy becomes useful.

The third Zen patriarch, a great Chinese sage from 606AD, said, "The great way is not difficult for those that have no preferences . . . to put one thing against the other is a disease of the mind."

This does not mean that we should not like chocolate more than vanilla. We all have preferences. However, when our happiness is fixed on "things" or on specific outcomes that we have a limited ability to change, we become unbalanced.

We always have the ability to change the tone and quality of our experience, to shift how we feel about what is happening.

We always have the ability to change the tone and quality of our experience, to shift how we feel about what is happening. Anchoring to our inner state to better handle what comes and goes is very much like traveling on a sailboat. When the wind is blowing in the direction that we want to go, it is great. It can be exciting when the wind becomes a gale or a storm, but it may also be dangerous, so we must be watchful. When there is not a puff of wind to be seen anywhere and the sea is still, then we must settle in and wait for it to change. Things are just the way they are; changing or accepting them are the only real solutions.

Buddha taught about the Two Truths—opposite realities that exist simultaneously, one within and around the other. The one truth is that the world is very real. We walk, talk, stand, and interact with it. There are consequences if we don't accept its seemingly solid reality. If we don't eat or if we run out into traffic without looking, the cause and effect realities of this "solid" world become apparent. This was the historically predictable world of Isaac Newton until Max Planck, Albert Einstein, Niels Bohr, and other scientists and thinkers cracked open the door with quantum physics; later, string theory blew it off its hinges.

As we examine our seemingly real world, it seems quite as it appears: solid and definable. Yet when we look more closely, we find that its solidity and even its predictability come into great question. This is the other truth. Even the most solid thing—your desk, for instance—is made of wood fibers that are made of molecules, which are made of atoms, which are made of particles, and so forth, smaller and smaller. At some point we have to accept that there is nothing there—just the illusion of something that is really just energy, vast space, and our awareness of it. From this perspective we can understand that Deep Happy comes from being more present in the smaller outer world without losing the thread of awareness of the big picture.

So now let's think about time. Much of our time is spent thinking about the past or the future—how things were or should have been; and what will or won't happen. Because of this, we often miss our third choice: what's here right now. Since the past is long gone and the future is an uncertainty, spending most of our time here in the present is a useful option. It is where everything is; it is the only place to find Deep Happy.

Each moment contains the essence of everything. Each moment is an entire universe when we let go of time.

Each moment contains the essence of everything. Each moment is an entire universe when we let go of time. The search for a true understanding of reality has permeated all knowledge. One single agreement that has emerged, whether it be from secular or transcendent sources, is that, without the separation and limitations of time and space, that the possibility exists that....we are all connected... To me this means that we are all connected to everything all the time, whether we know it or not. This view is shared by all esoteric spiritual traditions and modern physics.

This bigger connection is something I have explored all my life. When I was a little boy, about eight or nine years old, someone told me about infinity. I could not imagine something that had no beginning and no end. It was a great quandary for me. For months, when I was alone, I would close my eyes and try to feel the place that did not begin or end. I never told anyone about this.

One day, when I closed my eyes, I *got there.* I got to the place that neither began nor ended, and I thought, "Oh, so this is infinity." It was quite a normal and simple thing, really. At the time I just tucked it away and did not think of it in detail for a long while. It was a gentle moment that changed me the rest of my life, and whenever the word or idea of infinity came up, without realizing it, I would check to see if there was something there for me. Many years later, when I was thirty-seven and doing a long retreat in the Himalayas, the memory of that moment came to me. I realized that the experience had been a bridge—it connected me to what I can only think of as another time and place. That experience of the simplicity of infinite being has been a foundation and guide ever since. Interestingly, as I have told the story in my seminars and classes, I have met quite a few others who had this experience with infinity as children.

The deeper experience of happiness is something most of us have to get used to. It is easy to see a beautiful sunset, smell the fragrance of a flower, taste a wonderful meal, or even experience a sublime "ah-ha" moment, but how much can we allow each of the moments to nourish and change us? Deepening the experience of each moment does not need to take time; just a flash of awareness, even in the midst of doing other things can create a seemingly timeless interlude. Learning to take pleasure and beauty into our marrow is an important part of our journey back to ourselves and to Deep Happy.

I love the sky. Its ever-changing nature, clouds, and shades of color and light have always captivated me. When my son Namkai was a little boy, I used to point to a beautiful sky and say, "Isn't it beautiful!" He would look up briefly, or not, and mutter "Uh-huh," not really moving his attention from his book or video game. Now, at seventeen, he will exclaim, "Dad, look at that," pointing out a beautiful formation of clouds and taking the beauty into his own being.

Slowing down, even just for a moment, is the only prerequisite for taking pleasure and happiness into ourselves. When we see something beautiful, we can let the feeling of the colors and forms merge into our bodies. The next time you think of it, see if you can experience the colors and shapes as vibrations and sensations that are moving through you, nourishing you, filling you up with something divine.

When you taste something, let the taste expand into your whole body. When you make love, let the sensations of connection and pleasure move through you, opening and healing all the stuck and tight places with the physical sensations and feelings of bliss. Sex and physical pleasure can be very healing. When experiencing any kind of physical pleasure, notice how and where you limit the physical sensations. Over time, notice first the big and then the smaller places that are numb or have any reduced sensitivity anywhere on your body, gradually relaxing and expanding the good feelings. Eventually you will learn to experience all the nuances of pleasure and sensation in your whole body—and the vibrations of the universe with every cell. Even if you are not having physical intimacy, you can get used to letting pleasant sensations of any kind move through your body. If this process is difficult for you, please don't judge yourself—some things take time. The initial purpose of shutting down was to avoid pain, and your nervous system has to get used to being safe.

Several years ago I was teaching in the small Zendo in the rear of the property at the Providence Zen Center. By Sunday, we had spent several days doing meditation and Qigong practices. We were still and relaxed and in touch with the gentle rhythms and sensations of our bodies. It was spring, and warm. The forest around us was filled with new growth and energy. We could feel in our bodies the sounds of the gentle drops of rain on the pond, the buzzing of insects, and the whooshing of trees in the gentle breeze. When we allow nature to vibrate within us, the rhythms of the natural world can harmonize and soothe us, filling and nourishing our tight and tired places. Our bodies are as much from the natural world as any mountain, leopard, or river and have much to tell us when we listen.

Our bodies are as much from the natural world as any mountain, leopard, or river and have much to tell us when we listen.

"Okay, I can see that. But what if my body hurts and makes me miserable and prevents me from living my life?"

I have worked with patients for forty years. Most of them were in physical or emotional pain or had some difficulty with their body or mind not doing what they were supposed to do. When someone is in pain, the quality of that pain is always influenced by whatever held-in traumas and emotions are lingering beneath the surface. If someone has held-in anger, what comes out is anger. If they have grief or sadness, what come mixed with the pain are tears (or the struggle to hold the tears). The sensation of pain is physical and does not need to affect our state of being in all but the most extreme circumstances. Even in those most severe situations, we have the innate ability to drop into a state beyond the sensations of the body and find relief and peace. Even childbirth has the potential to be blissful and even orgasmic with training and preparation.

A great Tibetan Lama, Kusum Lingpa, once personally told me a story that was later confirmed by others who knew him. The Chinese had imprisoned him during Tibet's worst years of political chaos. The prison authorities wanted him to refute Buddhism and his beliefs. Kusum Lingpa had never been one to go quietly, and so had particularly irked the guards. When he refused, they decided to make an example of him.

They took him into a room and held his hand on a steel table. Using a large iron mallet, they smashed his fingers, one by one, each time asking if he would refute his faith. He lasted for three fingers before passing out, but using his meditative training and his strong belief, he was able to control his pain and help the healing of his hand, which was still deformed, but very animated while he told me the story.

This incident infuriated the guards even more. Kusum Lingpa's stubbornness and the quick healing of his hand made them even more determined to subdue his spirit. One moonless night they chained him to a stake that was driven into the frozen ground outside the prison gates. He was dressed only in his thin robes. Winters on the high Tibetan plateau are extremely cold. Temperatures of forty to fifty degrees below zero are not uncommon. With his leg chained to the stake, he was able to sit in meditation. The next morning when the guards found him, he was smiling, sitting in a ring of melted snow. He had used the Tibetan yogic techniques of "Tu Mo" to generate heat and a blissful meditation.

After that the guards left him alone. They seemed to realize that some of the Lamas had something more than belief; they had training and understanding in areas that transcended the normal and allowed them to connect to something unshakable. Even in those terrible and inhumane conditions, the abilities of the Tibetan Lamas influenced and transformed the attitudes of many of the guards.

These meditative and yogic practices are real and powerful. They have literally saved my life on several occasions, although nothing like being tortured in the frozen mountains of Tibet.

I have seen the simple process of inner meditative awareness change lives and even cure diseases as severe as cancer. On a simple level, just a few breaths into the lower abdomen can change our brain chemistry (as much as 85 percent of the body's serotonin is made in the gut). Working with deeply entrenched patterns and end-stage disease takes a great deal more time, training, and commitment, but is basically no more difficult.

In this chapter we have begun to lift the veil of who we are and some of the dynamics that keep us from being and expressing ourselves and that overshadow the part of us that is continually Deep Happy.

2

The Miracle That Is Us—the Big Picture

Every thing, every one, is a jar full of delight.

—Rumi

If quantum mechanics hasn't profoundly shocked you,
you haven't understood it yet.

—Niels Bohr

FEW OF US HAVE a clear understanding of our place in the universe and our purpose in this life. We might be able to construct an idea of our purpose and place philosophically or in our imagination, but these creative voyages do not bring the certainty of direct experience. Yet they are within the grasp of anyone who simply seeks them within the gentle stillness that resides in each of us.

Who are we? Where are we? And what the heck are we doing here? The complexity and sophistication of our current world has offered solutions, but the direction of these solutions has usually taken us further from the answer. Profoundly simple questions are best answered simply.

It is helpful for us to look at the nature of reality; to look deeper than we usually might to see how things are. If asked, most of us would say that the nature of reality is something we rarely think about, but we really do—and often! Any time we question the purpose of our lives, wonder if it is all worth it, or are surprised when something lost or unexpected wonderfully appears out of the blue, we are peering beneath the veil, touching our relationship to a deeper reality.

Science and religion have dug into this since before recorded history. This quest has filled all the libraries of the world. The thing that is most interesting and encouraging to me is that in the end everyone seems to reach the same point. The vocabularies and symbols may differ greatly, but when the highest and most profound end point of knowledge held by any discipline is distilled down to its essential truth, it looks pretty much the same: The material world, though difficult, pleasurable, and complex, is lacking any finite substance; time and space are only relative and limited constructions designed by us to traverse our relative world; and finally, there is a deeper infinite intrinsic reality that is the basis of all we know and beyond what most of us think we can imagine or experience.

Spiritual traditions describe this in varying ways as an underlying reality from which all things are made. The Tibetans use the Sanskrit word *Alaya,* which roughly translates as "the ground from which all arises." Many wisdom traditions also describe the material world as an illusion, real if we touch it or interact with it, but lacking in a finite existence if we break things down far enough to look at their essential structure.

Imagine looking at a lovely and colorful scarf. First we are attracted to the rich colors and delicate pattern in the weave. As we look more closely, our eyes notice the tightly interwoven threads. If we get out our magnifying glass we could inspect the threads themselves, noticing that each was made of smaller threads and that each of those was made from still smaller individual strands. Next we could get our old high school microscope out of the closet and discover that each strand was made of even smaller fibers. If we were really inspired, we could run over to our local research lab and borrow their electron microscope to see that the tiniest strands are also made of molecules which are made of atoms which are mostly empty space with just a few electrons and protons which themselves are mostly space with even tinier particles that are themselves mostly space.

An acquaintance of mine, Steve, used to work in the physics department at UCLA. He and I had several great talks. He spoke from the view of theoretical physics; I had the viewpoint of one knowledgeable about advanced Buddhist cosmology and other spiritual disciplines. One evening Steve and I were discussing the idea of infinity in his kitchen in Beverly Glen Canyon over several bottles of an interesting Malbec.

"You know," he said, "When we take infinity out of the equations, things are coherent and make sense, but if we include infinity, it shoots everything to hell."

He went on to explain that as long as he and his colleagues kept their experiments tangible, the outcomes followed suit. If they included the diverse possibilities of our multi-verse, the outcomes were unpredictable. Physics has not yet fully caught up to the reality that it has been attempting to describe.

The idea of infinity is not just a fanciful notion. When we move beyond the imaginary limitations of the sphere of awareness that we usually live in, the possibilities are also infinite. Let me give you an example of this, again from physics. We all have a passing knowledge of the immense power locked up within the atomic worlds. The terrible bombs dropped in Japan were small and relatively low-tech, yet the energy locked within those football-sized chunks of uranium was able to destroy whole cities. What Niels Bohr first proclaimed and most modern physicists agree on is that there is more free energy locked within a single centimeter of empty space (vacuum) than there is in all the matter in the universe. This is sometimes referred to as zero point energy.

When I first read that, my mind stopped for several days. The meaning and the immensity of it astounded me. This was my friend Steve's ironic point—that when we remove infinity from the equation, we may keep a certain order, but we also miss the most important part. This single deviation is one of the important reasons why science has not kept up with the widening of human consciousness that is currently changing the world from the inside, despite how unlikely it may look like from the outside.

When Niels Bohr and other physicists started paying close attention to subatomic particles in the 1930s, they noticed that the particles seemed to move into and out of reality.

Later on, they discovered that if you paid attention to the particles, they stayed right where they were, as if they sensed you.

Deep Happy Inner Practice

Take a moment and think about the idea of infinite energy.

Just imagine how much energy must be locked within the form of any physical thing you can think of. If a small amount can have such power, how much energy is locked up in your own body? Close your eyes, relax, and let yourself begin to feel the form of your body.

Then allow yourself to begin to notice the various sensations inside of it. Now let yourself gradually feel all the limitless energy or life force happily held within your physical structures. This energy, sometimes called life force, Qi, or Prana, is a savings account we can access just by remembering we have it. Allow yourself to open to it, letting it begin to flow freely throughout your body. Over time you will gradually experience more and more of the energetic reality within you. Eventually it will become second nature.

If you remember to do this, you will find that you will have all the energy already inside you that you will ever need—Deep Happy.

This is called the *Quantum Zeno Effect*, which was first stated in 1977 by George Sudarshan and Baidyanath Misra. The initial explanation for this is less mystical than it sounds: you cannot measure speed and location at the same time. This becomes compounded because many of the particles are actually moving in and out of our reality.

To me, this means that if subatomic particles, which are the basis of our material reality, respond to our thought, intent, and consciousness, then we as conscious beings can and do create reality and the life we are living in right now and every instant. To me, it is very unlikely that the entire universe hears our every thought and every feeling. This also means that it hears and responds to all our hopes, fears, and often conflicting simultaneous voices. When our hopes and dreams become more singular, so does the obvious response from the universe.

> Pick a flower on earth and you move the farthest star.
>
> —Paul Dirac

To make sense of this idea that the universe hears and responds to us, it is useful to let go of the concepts of size and time. Imagine that everything in the entirety of creation is just energy and light, and remember that you are, too. The energy that is you is equally part of the whole, without any kind of real separation or even individuality at this level except the point of awareness that is us. Play with this idea in your mind for a while. See where you get.

The basis of this concept has been the central theme in many current spiritually oriented books. If you focus on something, you can and will eventually get it. This is of course true. However if a part of us wants something and another part of us is afraid of that same something, then the great quantum universe hears and senses the tonal resonance of both voices and responds to both voices, and in a very real sense those voices cancel each other out. That's where the confusion comes in.

As we get used to just being ourselves and being present, the path of our life widens and progresses. It's not that we don't handle the responsibilities of our lives; it's just that we do so wide awake, allowing things to happen rather than forcing them. The process by which this occurs involves becoming more honest with our feelings and the details of our inner experience while at the same time using the external world for a reality check.

Deep Happy Inner Practice

Quietly relax in a comfortable position and think about something that you want but have had difficulty getting—perhaps a new job, a relationship, more friends, or even just some time off.

Quietly relax in a comfortable position and think about what you want. Allow your thoughts to arise organically and then consider each one. Think about it consciously and decide if you still want it. When you feel clear, refocus your goal without the interference of your doubts and secondary considerations. You will be surprised at how things change once your inner focus becomes simpler. Then begin to let your connection with all things expand, making it okay for the universe to hear and respond to you.

Developing a personal interaction with this bigger reality becomes really interesting when we finally decide to experiment with it. Certainly when the time comes to leave our bodies we will come face to face with it, but in the meantime it is a vitally interactive source that we can consciously call upon whenever we need help (we're already doing it all the time anyway). Eventually our need to ask disappears as we gradually accept our complete coherence with the big picture.

But in the meantime, what kind of help can we ask for?

I will give you some examples. In 1980 when I was developing the curriculum for an acupuncture school, there were very few books yet available offering the quality of detail we needed for the level of training we were approved by the State of California to provide. Many of the important sources were still only available in their native languages of Chinese, Japanese, and Korean. I discovered, quite by accident, that if I kept the files in my mind open—literally kept a space open where the needed information would be—that soon enough, the required material would just "drop in" and I would know the details of it and even see it as a three-dimensional form if I needed a visual diagram to understand it. Later on, when many of the topics were published in English, the "dropped-in" information would either match or be clinically more useful or advanced than what I found in print. Most of the clinical protocols that I now teach in my seminars to acupuncturists and other physicians came to me this way, and they have proven to be of very positive clinical significance to most practitioners who have learned and tried them.

Another example of this kind of help happened a few years ago. I was going through a very difficult period, and needed a break for my own healing and sanity. I decided that I would go up to the northern coast to Mendocino and get a room for several days by the ocean. I knew that it was a holiday weekend and all the rooms would likely be reserved. But when I tuned in, I got very specific guidance that if I listened carefully, I could trust things to work out. So, partly out of trust and partly out of curiosity, I headed north for the two-and-a-half-hour drive. As I entered the town of Mendocino, I began to get very specific feelings about how fast to go and which way to turn. I was directed to go specifically to a lovely inn overlooking the ocean. I went inside and inquired about a room.

"I'm sorry, but we're all full; it's a holiday, you know. Most of these rooms have been booked for months."

My inner guidance told me not to worry. "Get back in your car and drive north little bit." I drove slowly around town for about ten minutes until I got a strong feeling that I should go back to that same inn. I parked and went inside, and just as I reached the reception desk, the phone rang. As you may have already guessed, it was someone canceling a reservation. By following and trusting my inner guidance, I ended up with a lovely room where I could collect myself again, although the process I had just followed had created a very interesting beginning and reminded me how I needed to proceed to find balance in my life again.

When we begin to experiment and live from this idea of an interactive living universe, very surprising things can happen. It is deeply reassuring to know that we are never alone and never unsupported. When we trust this in our hearts, we are at the door of Deep Happy.

I had an old rusty red Dodge pickup truck that I used for hauling and moving. It had been sitting in my driveway for almost a year because I could not find the registration documents. Every month or so, I looked through every drawer and file in my house. Usually it was the same drawers and the same files, but also everywhere and anywhere else I could think of; it was my monthly bout of infuriation. Finally I decided to try a new tactic. I remembered that I could let the universe solve the problem. I literally said, "Okay universe, bring me the papers or show me where they are." In my mind I just let the whole thing go. Several days later, I drove my BMW station wagon into town. I had completely emptied the car of all trash and refuse before I left, and had also gone to a car wash where the car was completely cleaned, inside and out. I bought groceries and put them in a cardboard box from the store, carried the box out to the car, put it in the now very clean rear cargo section, and then drove straight home. As soon as I pulled in my driveway, I parked the car, went around and opened up the back, and lifted up the box of groceries. There, underneath the box was the registration to the red pickup truck. It was the same document that I had lost the year before. Stunned and amazed, I stood smiling and shaking my head. There are only two explanations for what had happened, but neither of them makes a lot of sense. Please keep in mind that this really happened.

One is that someone found my registration, somehow knew where I was parked, picked the lock on my car, and put the registration papers in the middle of my cargo section, which I did not notice when I put the box of groceries down.

The second explanation is that my documents appeared out of nowhere, pulled from the universe that responded to my request. Living in the box of "everyday expectation," it is so easy for us to forget that there are possibilities way beyond what we are used to. We are just like ice cubes floating in a giant sea, often feeling so alone, disconnected, and unsupported, yet surrounded by, as Meher Baba would say, "the all and the everything." Which possibility seems more believable to you?

When I first saw the future mother of my son, while shopping at the annual REI fall sale in Berkeley, I saw a tube of light connecting us. It was undeniable. I had to respond to it. In the end we were quite different people, but our destiny was to have our son, Namkai. The guidance was unmistakable.

My life has been one unlikely inner direction after another. A big one came in the late winter of 1984 when I felt another life change coming. The following spring, I gave up my acupuncture practice in Sonoma, California and moved to Monterey to study Chinese language for the summer. I trusted the strong inner feeling that had come over me eight months before, when it had told me that it was time for the next stage in my development.

My grandparents were missionaries in China and my father was born there. I was an acupuncturist and had lived and taught Chinese medicine, meditative arts, and culture. It seemed right for me to study Mandarin and finally go to China. I would be the fourth generation of my family to do so. However, that summer during my ten to twelve hours a day of studying Chinese, I realized that what I really wanted was a spiritual quest and I was not sure that I would find it in China. My inner guidance told me to keep going, so I did. One night, shortly after that, I was standing on the shore when a spontaneous prayer burst from my heart.

"Please take me to the place where I can get to the next level." Just as I heard those words in my mind, Tibetan symbols of light burst from my heart and seemed to fly out to the universe. At the time I didn't think anything of it—oddly, it seemed normal—but I kept the warmth of that moment in my heart for the next few days. One afternoon a week later, I was meditating in my yard, looking out at the ocean. Suddenly a face appeared in my inner vision, turned sideways, and disappeared. The face turned out to be that of a Tibetan teacher whom I was literally brought to several months later. My relationship to him turned out to be the most important pivoting point of my life; this book is dedicated to him. And how did I find him? I let the truth of my yearning come from my heart and sent it out for the universe to hear.

These things happen to me wherever I go. Several years ago I went to hear two African bands at the San Francisco Jazz Festival. The first one was great. The second group was apparently having a bad night, and after a couple of numbers, I was bored and decided to go out to the lobby of the theater. I started talking to a woman named Deborah who turned out to be the manager of the first group, Vieux Farka Touré, whose band leader is the son of Ali Farka Toure, the great legend of African guitar and Mali blues.

Deborah and I had a great conversation for about half an hour. It came out that some of the band members were having recurring malaria symptoms. I offered to go to their hotel the next day and treat them, and Deborah agreed. So late the next morning, I showed up at their hotel room in San Francisco. My treatments helped their symptoms, and through my broken French, their broken English, and

Deborah's translating, we had a great time. So much so that they invited me to go with them as their doctor to an African music festival called the Festival du Desert sixty miles north of Timbuktu, in Mali.

I went to Mali with my dear friend Christine. On the way home we wanted to stop in Morocco for a few days, and I decided to try an experiment. Eight years before I had met a Moroccan Sufi teacher, Sidi Ahmed Costas, while he was visiting United States. I had lost all of his contact information and only knew that he lived somewhere in Morocco. I suggested that we let the universe lead us to him, and Christine readily agreed.

My plan was that after we landed in the airport in Marrakech, we would go to the train station, which was adjacent to it, and walk around until someone came up to us and suggested a place where we should go. After about fifteen minutes, a smiling local teenage boy came up to us and asked if we were Americans. We replied that we were.

"Have you ever been to Fez?" he asked with great enthusiasm. "No, but we're about to buy tickets for there right now," we answered, smiling to each other.

We bought the tickets, and after a short wait, boarded the train. We did not have to wait long for what happened next. At the first stop, a well-dressed Moroccan gentleman entered the compartment and sat down in the corner across from us by the window. He was reading a book written in English, *Buddha in the Suburbs,* and I thought to myself, "I must speak with this person." We were soon engaged in conversation, and I asked the man if he had heard of Sidi Ahmed Costas.

"Yes," he replied, surprised. "He's a good friend of mine, but I haven't seen in several years and am not sure how to reach him. I do know that he still lives in Fez, though."

Christine and I looked at each other. We were both pretty amazed that we had found not only the right train and the right car but the right *person* to lead us to my friend. We had found the city were Costas lived, and we were on our way there. Christine and I wondered what would come next. Again, we did not have to wait long.

At the very next stop, a young woman entered our compartment and sat down next to me. Shortly after the train started to move again, she began conversing in French with the gentleman across from us. After about ten minutes, he looked up and said,

"She knows Costas! He is her advisor at the university!"

By that evening, we had my friend's phone number and email address. He joined us for dinner the next evening, though as a Sufi and a mystic, he was not at all surprised at how we had found him.

This book and several others could be filled with stories like this. Long ago I decided to live my life in this way, trusting and communicating my needs to a bigger reality and most importantly, being open to it. We are all connected in this way and we all have these experiences. Most of the time, though, we doubt, ignore, or simply don't notice them. We are used to saying, "Oh, this worked out well," or "I just got a great idea." But from the perspective I'm talking about does it really matter whether the idea came from my brain, my intuition, or the sacred/quantum universe? Are these sources really any different?

Most indigenous people use signs from nature for guidance. I have found this to be a highly interactive and useful process. When we have symbols that are important to us, the universe can use our awareness of them and their appearance to give us information.

I have always had a close connection with animals. My house is a furry and feathery collection of dogs, cats, and birds. Having them around reminds me of the essential essence of the natural world, which helps me maintain inner balance for the work that I do. However, there are two specific animals that I have an unceasing connection with; they show up when it's important for me to notice or recognize something. Crows (and to a certain extent birds in general) and rabbits have always felt like friends and guides to me. I will talk more about rabbits in my chapter on the heart.

In the early 1990s, I went back to Nepal for five months to finish a series of meditative practices. I spent the first half of my retreat in a small apartment on the outskirts of Boudhanath, and the second half up in the high mountains of the Himalayas, about twenty miles south of Mount Everest. During that solitary period in the mountains, I would typically do meditative practices for twelve to eighteen hours a day. For part of each day, when the weather permitted, I practiced outside my little cabin that was perched on a ledge at an altitude of about thirteen thousand feet and about five thousand feet above the valley below. Several times a day I heard whooshing sounds above my head. It was a large flock of crows flying thousands of feet above me, putting on the air brakes of their wings before slowing to land on my little edge.

The crows were practically my only visitors, and I became very familiar with the dynamics of their flock. I noticed that their leader was an older crow and that a younger crow was trying to take over his position. They were my only diversions, and I came to know them well. Each time the younger crow aggressively moved toward the older crow, I tossed a tiny pebble in his direction to show my support for the older fellow. It only took a few incidents like that for the older crow to accept me as an ally. Each time the flock appeared while I was outside, the older crow stayed somewhat near me; if I was inside, he would *kaw* for me until I came out. For those several months I became an honorary member of their flock. Himalayan crows are larger than the ones we have here in the United States. They are almost as big as chickens and have gray necks and heads and shiny black bodies. They were powerful and smart, and I came to feel a part of them; they became a family for me during my solitary retreat in that cabin.

Without the normal elements of distraction and intense activity of life, it is easier to follow the life of the natural world. When inner and outer stillness meet in the simplicity of nature, communication with any life form becomes effortless. But even in the complexity of our normal twenty-first-century lives, the universe is speaking to us every moment.

My son Namkai and I used to live in a house on a tidal creek, by a marsh, in Marin County. Like most of our neighbors along the creek, we had a small dock. One day while looking out the kitchen window across the water to the marsh, I saw five big white egrets perched on the railing of my neighbor's dock. From my viewpoint, they were lined up exactly in a row. The next day at the same time, I looked out the window and saw five big black buzzards lined up exactly as the five white egrets had been the day before. I took this as a sign that the energy of our lives was moving into a more difficult direction, and it was.

A tough year later, almost to the day, my son and I were out by the pool when we heard a strong fluttering sound from the altar in the open lanai next to where we were standing. We went inside to find that a young hawk had settled right on the small Tibetan carpet that covered the top of the altar. Without thinking about it, I walked over to the altar, gently slid my hands under the carpet, and lifted it, holding the carpet with the hawk. The young hawk did not fight or even seem alarmed. We were both amazed—we could feel the wild bird's power. We knew it was something important. My first thought was to keep the hawk as a pet, but then I realized that we had to let him go. As we let him fly away, I knew that the difficulties of the last year would change. Our life got much better from that day on.

Great teachers have always spoken of paying attention. Whether it is looking for a sign, trusting God to hear your prayers, or speaking directly to the universe, the teachings from all the great spiritual and native lineages confirm that we are not alone and that someone/something is listening. For example, in the 1930s, Paramahansa Yogananda was one of the first great Indian yogis to achieve "notoriety" in the United States. He had supreme and sometimes humorous trust in the divine. He knew with the utmost certainty that whatever he asked for would be granted. In his autobiography, he writes about leaving his house with forty-five minutes left before his train would leave from the station. He announced to God, with the greatest humility, "Lord, I need three rupees for the train, and I need it within forty-five minutes. Thank you." He always had the money by the time he got to the train. He had no doubt about it!

One of the most important benefits of this work is getting that we are infinitely supported and can directly experience ourselves as a part of the living universe.

The first step is to experiment in little ways to let the universe support us. When my wife Conde and I were planning for our wedding, we were in great consternation about what to serve and how to serve it. At some point we decided we needed someone to take charge of the barbecue, and I suggested that we let the universe provide. Within five minutes, a friend called me on the phone. When I mentioned to him what we needed, he said, "Oh, I love doing that."

This might seem like a mundane example, but in the context of all the possibilities, it is anything but mundane. Just as each of the trillion cells in our body need specifics from the whole to flourish, so do we. If each little cell in our body can make demands, why can't we demand from our bigger body, the universe?

One of the most important benefits of this work is getting that we are infinitely supported and can directly experience ourselves as a part of the living universe.

I used to listen to a radio doctor in the San Francisco area who said frequently on his programs that there are no miracles. We lived near each other, and occasionally I would see him in the video store. We had several heated debates about natural medicine. He would always say, "Miracles are not scientific!"

But every miracle is scientific. How could it not be? Isn't science just an organized version of curiosity? Isn't disbelief the epitome of an unscientific attitude?

Ninety-three billion miles from earth is a ball of fire eight hundred thousand miles wide. It has been burning for six billion years or so, and inside it is a black hole. All life in our solar system depends on this ball of fire. That seems like a miracle to me. Several hundred thousand light years from earth out in space, there is a black hole six hundred light years across. Relatively near it is a quasar that is a thousand times bigger and brighter than our sun. That's a pretty big ball of fire! Scientists couldn't figure out why the entrance to the black hole was not heating up, and then they discovered a B-flat tone was emanating from the black hole. Several years ago, *Scientific American* had a picture of the waves emanating from the black hole. Just as ripples move out in a pond when a pebble is thrown in, the ripples of this B-flat tone were visible in the photograph; they were ten light years apart. New developments in physics and cosmology are showing that the universe is in fact held together with electromagnetic fields and currents and enormous seas of plasma. Scientists have identified a plasma tornado two trillion kilometers long! Too bad there are no miracles!

The human body has at least one hundred trillion cells—maybe a lot more. It depends on who's counting. Each of those hundred trillion cells has a hundred thousand bonding sites on its surface. Inside each cell are thousands of metabolic functions going on every second; each cell is in communication with millions of other cells. And somehow, it all works together pretty well, most of the time. What we can see from all this is that though things get infinitely bigger and infinitely smaller, we are always in the middle, which is the place of power, connection, and balance. And since time and space have limited meaning in the bigger reality, we can trust that we are as important and connected in this universe as any quasar or solar system. Just as our complex bodies function automatically, so does the complexity of our connection to the universe function in and around us all the time. We just have to remember or choose to notice the details of the reality we want to be in, realizing we may need a transition period. Like clouds parting on a gray day to reveal a blue sky and blazing sun, the wonders of the universe are waiting for our awakened heart to beckon them.

3

Who We Are

It's pretty hard to tell what brings happiness.
Poverty and wealth have both failed.
—Kin Hunnard

Who Did You Say I Was, Again?

Contrary to popular mythology, happiness is the intrinsic biological state and awareness that underlies all that we are. Once we drop below our personality, learned programming, and adapted referencing to time and space, our natural resonance is Deep Happy.

As we peel back the all the layers of numbness and habit, eventually all that remains is the simple pristine awareness of being.

Developing Vitality

Vitality comes as we free the physical body from our old patterns. As we learn to experience Deep Happy, we are not just opening the body; we are also changing the tone of an entire universe of little conscious beings inside of us. We are a mobile and intelligent fortress of at least one hundred trillion individually conscious cells (90 percent are bacteria, yeast, fungus, and so forth and are made up of microscopic colonies called micro-biomes). In our heads we also have at least one hundred trillion or so neurons and six times that many glia, which fill the space around the neurons and are now thought to be important indicators of intelligence. Einstein's brain had the usual amount of neurons, but massive amounts of glia. Dolphins and whales have a ratio of seven or eight glial cells to neurons. Humans have a ratio of five or six. In addition to our five main senses, we have subtle senses involving electromagnetic fields, direction, intuition, and certain kinds of direct inner perception. All of these are focused on accurately recording what is going on around us and sending smoke signals to the brain and motor nerves so that we can respond in ways that will assure our survival and quality of life. This gigantic amount of activity goes on, for the most part, without our conscious knowledge. Though it's important to mention here that if we choose to do so, we can interact with these senses and focus on any part of us—no matter how small. Just like the captain of a huge ocean liner who would rarely go down to the engine room or kitchen but could if he or she wanted to, so can we.

As we peel back the all the layers of numbness and habit, eventually all that remains is the simple pristine awareness of being.

Besides the intricacies inside our bodies, we have a complex outer layer of receptive and expressive functions we call personality. We play our personalities like a musician plays his piano or her cello. Our personalities express our intermingled experiences and continually stream our genetic histories and the filtered referencing of our higher consciousness. We are like symphonies, with all the different parts of us being the individual instruments. Like a box of badgers and kittens, the various aspects of ourselves either quarrel or speak in a unified voice. First recognizing and becoming familiar with them and then untangling these inner voices is an important process for developing personal coherence and unifying who we are and what we want to do with our lives.

Most of the personality is anchored to the physical body. This connection is only partially related to the brain, and is in fact embedded into a complex web of physiology that spans the level of nanobiology up through the chemical, electrical, hormonal, and subtler energetic systems of the body. (Current research indicates that these electromagnetic flows of our body—the Chinese called them *Jing Luo* or channels—are intimately connected to the gigantic intergalactic flows of electromagnetic energy that spin galaxies and connect the entire universe.) These filters also color our response to the events that appear to us each moment, constantly limiting, editing, or extending what we understand to be reality through the filter of personality, expectation, and habit.

The complexity inherent in our personalities is often at odds with who and how we want to be, or even more importantly, how we see ourselves. A few weeks ago, I was working with a young college student, Serena, who wanted help because she felt she wasn't doing well academically or socially. Yet when she described her life, she told me that she had good grades, had recently ended an abusive relationship, had found a job in an extremely thin job market, and had just been accepted for a month-long internship in Europe. When I pointed out that she was handling her life better than most of her fellow students, she paused and sheepishly agreed.

"I guess you're right; I didn't think of it that way," she said. "I'm so used to seeing myself as not being very together."

How many times have we overreacted to something someone said to us and later wondered why, or shut down in the presence of someone we wanted to get to know but just couldn't think of anything sensible to say? These kinds of responses indicate that we have triggered patterns of protection and denial that have been imprinted in us. Traditionally these kinds of issues are seen as emotional, but they can be understood from a much broader perspective of deeper physiology and even karmic tendencies.

My understanding of personality is still evolving. Many of my most important insights came from studying how intensive spiritual disciplines affect people and how they affect our minds, our diseases, and our lives.

I lived for much of seven years in a bustling and very funky Tibetan town just outside of Kathmandu in Nepal. By the time I left, there were over forty monasteries clustered around the Great Stupa of Boudhanath, which is a very large, sparkplug-like structure that grandly stands in the center of the town that grew up around it over a thousand years. Stupas are built from an ancient, esoteric science and are designed to radiate different kinds of energy out into the world. The one in the town of Boudhanath radiates the energy of enlightenment. As such, Boudhanath has been a holy pilgrimage place for Nepalese, Tibetans, Buddhists, and spiritual seekers of all kinds for many centuries. Besides the monks, Lamas, and Rinpoches (high teachers) who live there, pilgrims come from all over the world to study, meditate, and learn the sacred transformational practices that, in the Buddhist tradition, liberate us from the suffering of our lives until we remember our own enlightened essence.

The advanced versions of these many transformative practices can take decades to fully master and integrate. Many people come to Boudhanath to study with the teachers who live there or visit there yearly. A large majority of these ardent seekers do several hours of study and meditative work each day. Many also go up to the mountains for longer, solitary retreats of months or years. The atmosphere makes it as easy to do daily meditative practices there as it is to *not* do them here in our busy world.

To become a teacher in that system, just like any other, one moves through a progressive individual training. The culmination is the three-year retreat or its equivalent. Three years, three months, and three days of twelve- to eighteen-hour-a-day intensity causes aspirants to drop through the habitual patterns that keep us from the direct experience of our essential infinite nature.

I had the opportunity to know many who had gone through this process. Some I got to see the before and after. One thing surprised me more than anything else and forever changed the way that I understand spirituality. Very often the personalities of those entering the training were not greatly changed through this arduous and sublime experience. Whatever personality flaws they had going in, they often still had coming out.

Inevitably, though, there was something else that had changed about them, an inner part that *shimmered* and was much clearer and more present than before. The gap between these two aspects was so obvious and intriguing to me that a good part of my interest and research since then has been to work out exactly what I had observed and to develop a map that could be used clinically for my clients who wanted to open spiritually—and who wanted to just be happy.

This was the beginning of my study of trying to deeply understand what spirituality means, practically, within the relationship between our physical body and our consciousness. For the next few years I used various methods in my investigations. I physically observed my patients and friends, did intensive meditative practice myself, read everything I could, studied with transformative teachers, physicians, and scientists from all over the world, and talked with anyone who would share their meditative experiences with me. Since most of my medical clients were either yogis or those who had come from all over the world to study and practice, I was able to learn a great deal from them, especially using subtle methods of diagnosis and observation from Asian medical systems. When I combined these experiences in the East with what I had previously learned of the physiology of emotions, Oriental medicine, neurophysiology, biofeedback, meditation, Qigong, and many other therapies, I felt like I had finally found important pieces of the puzzle. Over the last twenty-five years, I have gradually developed and simplified it all into a system that I work with and teach to others at various levels. When I give trainings for acupuncturists, physicians, psychologists, and healers, I present a very detailed system based on an East/West model of physiology. For non-medical people I present just the essentials, as I am doing in this book. I will try to give you a simple overview. Are you ready?

Part One

Our bodies come from our ancestors. Through the lineages of our mothers and fathers, we get the physical traits of height, weight, build, and coloring. We also get family quirks of personality and impulse. These influences are in the body, mind, and belief system. Even things like emotions and mental abilities are largely the result of physical influences in the body that shift and balance the function of the brain, nervous and hormonal systems, and subtle energetic complexes. We all take credit or blame ourselves for how we are, but much of us is pre-programmed before we even have a name.

Mice can be taught to run a maze. Each successive generation can run the maze more and more easily until a generation is born that can do the same maze without even learning it. They just know it. It is in them. We are the same; only for us the maze is life. We have huge data banks of inbred tendencies, tastes, inclinations, and even, like the mice, information.

In my observation, this is not just a genetic passing of the torch, although that is certainly a major part of it. We also get a great deal of what I call learned patterns of the family, some of which are often misdiagnosed as genetic traits. Especially as infants and children, our survival depends on learning how those around us do things.

In the early 1970s I was working in pediatrics as an orderly at a large hospital in Santa Barbara. A five-day-old baby, who had been in isolation because of an infection, was being held by his father. As father and son moved up the hall toward me, I happened to notice that the baby's right shoulder was held a bit higher than his left. Then my eyes shifted to the father, whose right shoulder was held in exactly the same tension pattern. Five days and already the little guy was taking on the family style and the weight of the world.

The traits that get passed down to us from our families are not just the obvious things like how to walk and eat and talk like we come from Brooklyn. We also learn how those around us feel or don't feel about things, how they respond to certain situations, how they think, and more fundamentally how they creatively express or contain who they are. Our first instinct is to be like them.

All of these influences create patterns that affect us in physical and observable ways. The gifted writer and thinker Rupert Sheldrake describes this connection as Morphogenic Fields, connections in consciousness that unite families and groups of people and things through time and space. Probably our ancestral connections are much more pervasive than we know.

In Chinese medicine, this physical link to the past is connected to the kidneys, not specifically in their function in processing fluids, electrolytes, and so forth, but energetically. We understand them to "pass the momentum of the ancestors."

This may sound like some anecdotal myth, but this ability of the kidneys is clearly discernible with the Oriental system of diagnosis and other subtle methods of assessment.

Pulse diagnosis is one of the most interesting of these techniques. We have all been to the doctor and had our pulse taken. Your doctor, or more probably his nurse, felt the pulse at your wrist to determine the rate of your heartbeat, whether it was too fast, too slow or in some way different from the norm. Your heart may have also been listened to for any irregularities in intensity, rhythm or function. The Asian systems look for these things as well, but the pulse can give us a more integrated view.

This system of diagnosis and observation, with time and training, allows the practitioner a high degree of detailed assessment. It illuminates the general and specific function of each of the organs; how they are working together; inner and outer influences that may be adversely affecting them; and the overall function of the body as a whole—all without laboratories or expensive diagnostic equipment and at no cost but a few minutes of the doctor's time. It can uncover some truly surprising information.

It is possible to tell the year that certain physical or emotional traumas happened, and the area of the body where the effects still linger. Through the years I have developed a teachable protocol for describing the emotional personality of each parent from the pulse, and the resultant effects and patterns in their children. This particular aspect is felt on the right and left kidney pulses and verifies what the *Nei Jing,* an ancient classic of Chinese medicine, proclaimed over two thousand years ago.

From the pulse we can also discover and accurately monitor the history of the disease and its response to therapy in real time, again at minimal cost.

In the early 1980s, I was the acupuncturist at Esalen Institute in Big Sur, California. Esalen is a wonderful retreat and conference center that rests on the cliffs overlooking the Pacific. People come from all over the world to rest, find new focus for their lives, and study with teachers from a wide assortment of disciplines.

My clinic was in a big house overlooking the ocean. I could look out the windows to see otters floating on their backs and dolphins and whales swimming by. One day a young woman came to me complaining of menstrual problems. We talked for a short while and I took her pulse. After a few minutes I asked her, "What happened when you were fifteen years old?"

She looked confused. "I was raped," she said, and looked down.

"I'm sorry, I don't think you were. What really happened?"

She looked angry for a moment, and then her face relaxed.

" . . . My brother and I were only nine months apart. We lived in the country with not much to do and were both very hormonal. One day we just did it with each other. It was so abhorrent to me afterward that I just pushed it away and never thought about it again."

I wouldn't usually recommend suggesting to a woman that she wasn't raped, but when I felt this woman's pulse, I detected an obstruction in the pelvic area but no anger. I don't believe anybody could ever be raped and not harbor some sense of rage. These things can stay with us, slowly changing how we see and respond to the world around us. For my client, just remembering for the first time in fifteen years what had happened to her began to free her body from the grip of denial that she placed on it after that afternoon with her brother. Her pulse changed almost immediately and she began to have a slight cramping. I suggested that she go home and put heat on her tummy. The next day she told me that she felt great. I ran into her a year later and she happily reported that her periods were normal. This is such a good example of how we hold in our body all that is unfinished and that as soon as we accept and release the experience of it, we can heal. Let's look at the next step of who we are.

Part Two

There is another part of us—a part that did not come from our parents. It is our connection to our current level of consciousness, which is who and how we are spiritually. This part of us is anchored into the physical body through the heart, which allows the frequency of our consciousness to integrate and express our spiritual essence into the body. It also creates an emotional foundation for love and the expression of warmth and compassion. The heart and its connection to the higher states give us an interesting perspective on what it means to be deeply alive and Deep Happy. More detail about this later in Chapter 5.

The organ and energetic system of the heart is a wonderful channel that both sends and receives. It connects the duality of our three-dimensional world with the direct experience of the non-dual, non-local realms. Non-local means beyond time and space—in this sense the heart is the bridge that connects us in time to our seemingly physical world while simultaneously being aware of the bigger picture. This is a good thing! It is so helpful when the unified experience of these two realities becomes viable, allowing access to action guided by insight and knowledge.

Part Three

It is the union of the heart and kidneys—the mixing of ancestral wisdom with the pervasive spiritual awareness and insight that come together within the core of our physical and energetic bodies—that allows us to be fully human and Deep Happy. Martial artists are not fully beginners until they reach the black belt level, because they haven't learned the full system. Once they have learned and integrated all the parts, they can fully express the whole system through their personal style. In that same way, as the ancestral and physical heritage and wisdom that are channeled through the kidneys meet octaves of consciousness and spiritual awareness channeled through the heart, we can finally assume a level of integration that is the basis of real human development.

This system is not religious, though some may interpret it that way. It is not Christian or Buddhist, Sufi or Hindu, yet the esoteric traditions of any of them will have similar descriptions in their own language using their own techniques and practices. Over several millennia, esoteric, meditative, and yogic disciplines have become intertwined with religion. The attitudes of humility, compassion, simplicity, and selflessness were fostered by these established traditions. These attitudes became a vital foundation for any of their spiritual practices because they created a subtlety of deep healing and balance, naturally aligning the physiology and mental state of the practitioner and smoothing obstacles for developmental success. It was often only at the most rarefied level of these traditions that the highest teachings were available. The lower echelons usually espoused limited doctrines meant more to influence and control than to enlighten. Though here I must add that these traditions also taught that purity of the individual's intent would inevitably protect and in the end guide them to whatever source they needed. In the ancient way, solitary yogis would attract by subtle means those who would be receptive to their teachings, and seekers would be guided to the next level of their training.

We can begin to see that the issues of human limitation are simply patterns of personality, ancestry, habit, and karmic tendency; they have a clear and specific physiology. These issues are what all the preparatory spiritual practices are designed to heal. Once we understand and integrate the subtle physiology that these practices represent, we will have a new basis for developing creative solutions—not just for treating diseases, but for understanding and solving many societal problems as well.

It's important to understand how disruptive traits are held within our biological and subtle energetic structures. When we uncover the details about how they act as restraints or lenses, inhibiting or amplifying the simple expression of infinite consciousness through biological form, we will be able to change our medical systems to actually help society shift to a vibrant and freely interactive state of being.

The intent is not to "re-create" anyone in some predetermined way—quite the contrary. If during a storm a tree falls across the creek behind my house and stops the water from flowing, removing the tree only allows the water to again flow whereever it would naturally go. We are just opening the possibilities. As with any clinical or personal assessment, we must withhold any moral, religious, or private judgment from our work with others (or even ourselves). By being pragmatic and open, we will get to unexpected places and ways of being that we didn't even know were possible.

Offering of help and direction without the need for control or recognition is true compassion.

Offering of help and direction without the need for control or recognition is true compassion.

The process of understanding personality, especially as an interactive carrier of karmic tendencies, can be greatly accelerated by getting to know interesting and highly developed people. In Nepal, in those years, it was fairly easy to develop personal relationships with the Lamas. Most had begun their training as small children, and as would be expected, each was completely unique. Most had a deep sense of humor, and many taught profound lessons of compassion with each word and nuance. Writing this brought tears to my eyes remembering the specialness of it all. Yet at the time it all seemed so normal. My main teacher, Dabsang Rinpoche, spent several decades in retreat, yet he was still be able to tell stories of Tibetan bandits, and with a twinkle in his eye brag about how many times he had fallen off his horse as a boy in Kham, a region in eastern Tibet. He had a wonderful sense of humor and a softness often belied by his high position and sometimes stern appearance.

One time shortly after I arrived from the West, I offered to give Rinpoche a shoulder massage. He agreed, and I moved behind him and started to massage his shoulders. Suddenly, an impish part of me took over. Trying not to give my intentions away, I moved my hands down and suddenly began to tickle his ribs. He leapt up in glee, spun around, went into a fighter's crouch, and pretended to come at me, laughing. The monks were aghast! They had never seen anyone tickle their Rinpoche before.

Knowing and being connected to our ancestral heritage is important. Tibetans, even if they have lost their land and country, know their land, food, religion, clothing, and history. They know what they have and who they are—or what they have lost (though this is fading with young Tibetans living in Lhasa and other cities in Tibet). This historic sense is an important foundation for anyone's emotional stability. I believe this is a primary reason the emotional milieu is so chaotic in many Westerners.

Besides the Tibetan system, I have also had the opportunity to train and practice with several Taoist and Qigong lineages, as well as Zen, Vipassana, Hindu, Tantric, Advaita, and Sufi traditions. The style and flavor of these different esoteric Asian and Middle Eastern systems is similar in purpose, style, and to some extent, physiology. The thing that separates them most clearly is lineage.

The real meaning of lineage is not well understood in the West. In spiritual traditions where we receive training in a particular form of practice or understanding, we are not just learning something tangible. In a very real sense, we are entering into the mind and energy stream of all those who've come before and reached a perfected state of accomplishment using that particular system. This is the real value of connecting to a practice lineage because it opens us to the wisdom and guidance that comes within the humility of our receptivity. Part of the process that comes with seriously entering any of these traditions is a deep commitment and personal acceptance of this union. This kind of connection can be simple, or it can involve a detailed energetic aligning with the particular tradition involved. Once this connection to lineage is made, it becomes a palpable and pragmatic source of strength, direct knowledge, and even protection. I experience an active connection with several Tibetan, Taoist, and Qigong lineages, but it's important to note that you do not need to be aligned with any particular tradition to evolve or develop spiritually. Each of us has his or her own lineage of ancestors and inner helpers. Trust what interests you and where you are guided above all other influences!

This idea of lineage is not just faith or belief, although these elements certainly strengthen the viability of lineage. On the contrary, it is something that becomes a part of us, perhaps a little like a computer program working in the background, only guiding and focusing with a felt personality and a distinct tone that we can freely utilize or leave alone as we wish. Some years ago there was a very charismatic Danish teacher named Ole Nydal who taught Tibetan practices internationally. His lineage was that of the Karmapa, the spiritual head of the Kagyu order. At one point there arose around him a great deal of controversy. Some doubted his authentic lineage connection. But when I meditated in his center's meditation room in Copenhagen, I experienced the exact tone and energy as I had when I meditated in the Karmapa's own room at his home monastery in Sikkim. The connection was undeniable. I am not an ordained Tibetan teacher, though I do have permission to teach in several Taoist and Qigong lineages. Often, though, when I am teaching I feel the lineages of all of my teachers flowing through me.

Healing Our Own Lineage of Family

As I have written previously, a certain part of what makes up our personalities comes from our families. Many of these traits are beneficial; some are obstacles that we must recognize and transform into experience and wisdom. These become great gifts. Some will let go on their own as we grow and develop coherence; some of the deeper ones might need help. There are many healing natural systems that work well on behavior and mood, including acupuncture, neurofeedback and stimulation, homeopathy, Chinese and other herbal systems, nutrition, Qigong and, of course, meditation. I have used these methods to help thousands of people with issues like anxiety, depression, and creative blocks. As we heal our inner limitations, we can experience living within the supporting streams of our ancestral families and our higher consciousness.

Many people would rather not reconnect to family lineages that brought them heartbreak, abuse, and neglect. But there are at least two things about this to consider. The first, I believe, is that our free will and consciousness brought us to this very life. Not that we wanted to be abused—we want to have the profound opportunity to accomplish the karmic lesson with which we can connect to our deep selves no matter what is going on around us. The second thing to keep in mind is that all parents, even the worst, have a biological love and connection to their offspring. In my experience, it is there, hidden within even the most hardened personalities. I would even go so far to say that at a primal level, the pain of emotional or physical separation from your child is as wrenching for the parent as it is for the child, if not more so. Beneath the crazy personalities of our families and ancestors there exists a powerful field of love, hope, and support. The energetic or morphogenic connection is an organic, living stream that connects each of us to all that came before. And some say to all that is to come.

Trust becomes the ability to see who someone is, rather than holding blind expectations about them.

At an essential level, all of our ancestors love us from their deepest hearts. This powerful love exists in a continuum outside of time in the realm of mind and biology, beneath and beyond personality. It is a real and stable source that we can tap into for energy, love, healing, and knowledge. It is powerful to feel and open to the supporting field of our ancestors—not their disturbed personalities, but their deepest essence.

At some point, to move on, we all have to drop the veil of blame and victimization and begin to see the terribly wounded hearts of those who have harmed us. It may seem intolerable to ask this of anyone who has truly suffered at the hands of others, but forgiveness is the only path to real healing; our healing. As we open our eyes and hearts to see the imprinted pain and the unrelenting forces that drove those who have hurt us, we can begin to find ways to at least understand them and eventually forgive them.

It is critical for us to keep in mind that forgiving does not in any way condone anything bad that was done to us or anyone else. Forgiving means accepting that whatever was done to us was not about us, even though each beating or abandonment seemed so directly personal. It truth, the perpetrators' actions came from the furnaces of their own torment and had nothing to do with us. We were just a hanging target at their shooting range. We can widen our understanding to forgive others for their deep wounds, acknowledging them as fellow humans but keeping vigilant about recognizing the feeling and tone of our wounds so we never have to put ourselves in the same position of vulnerability ever again.

The real teaching here is to see that the most important part of us is always Deep Happy.

Trust becomes the ability to see who someone is, rather than holding blind expectations about them.

Years ago, when I was in my twenties, I used to go to Magic Mountain outside of Los Angeles and ride the biggest roller coaster again and again until I could keep my meditation even during the steepest drop. For many of us, families have the same purpose.

The real teaching here is to see that the most important part of us is always Deep Happy.

Deep Happy Inner Practice

Connecting to Your Lineages

After relaxing and calming your mind, sink into the totality of yourself. Begin to feel the influences from both of your parents. Let the bottom of your left foot connect up to your left kidney. (The kidneys are right and left of the mid-line above the bottom of the ribs on the back.) This is a reference to the momentum and lineage of your mother and her family. Reflect on the feeling and personality of your mother's family, and make a connection from your left kidney down through your left leg to your left foot, extending out infinitely like the roots of a tree. Let all the nourishing, loving, and informational influences of your mother's entire family connect to you as a source of strength and knowledge for you to call on whenever you might want or need it.

Do virtually the same process for the lineage of your father's family. Let the bottom of your right foot connect up to your right kidney. This connects you to the momentum and lineage of your father and his family. Let yourself reflect on the feeling and personality of your father's family, extending out infinitely like the roots of a tree from the bottom of your foot. Let all the nourishing, loving, and informational influences of your father's entire family connect to you.

For those who are adopted, use the same process. You have a choice—because you are an accepted part of your adopted family, you can do this practice with each of your lineages. You can also choose to explore the genetic and energetic connection that still exists with your birth parents. Here you must be sensitive enough to discover the energy of your biological lineage, since you may not remember them. Let any positive undiscovered abilities or traits emerge as vital possibilities.

You can also let the positive influences of any non-blood caregivers who raised you connect to you in the same way.

The Real Us

Even as your body has changed, there is an essential "you" that has been constant over the course of your entire life. This timeless part of ourselves is the foundation of all that we call *me* and is also where we find Deep Happy.

Deep Happy Inner Practice

Who Is the Unchanging You?

Take a minute and think back to the "you" that has always been the same. The "you" that has never changed, that is same as you remember being when you were six, twelve, twenty-five, and so forth up until now. Who is that you? As the awareness of this unchanging you emerges, experiment with letting it be part of you during your day. Notice when you feel more or less than part of yourself. How do you feel when you're more connected to it? Play with it.

If We Are Not Our Body, Who Are We?

We know that we have a body. It is what moves us around and gives us the experiences of pleasure and pain and everything in between. But most of us would not say that we *are* a body. Why not? Because most of us have at least a vague understanding that we are also something else—something beyond the body. The Buddhists have an interesting meditative experiment for this.

Deep Happy Inner Practice

Are We Our Body?

Imagine that one of your arms disappeared. Would you be less of a person without that limb?

What if both arms and both legs were missing, like the knight in the Monty Python movie? Would you be less of a person then?

How about if you had only one lung, one kidney, one ear, one breast, or one testicle?

Would you be less of a person?

If not, then the question is: If we are not the body, then who are we?

Think about this for a while.

I recently attended a funeral. The deceased was my new brother-in-law, whom I had not had the chance to meet before he died, so I didn't get know him as a living person with breath, feelings, and personality. It was interesting to see his body in the open casket, dressed in a suit, hair combed—he was all ready for his own funeral, but nobody was home. The body was empty of life, of consciousness. But exactly what part of us *does* fill the body? Who is the "us" that comes into our physical form before birth and then leaves when the body is of no use to us anymore?

As you read through the rest this book, be aware of the part of you that is not your body. See if you can become aware of the you that inhabits your space suit of skin and bones.

4

Getting Used to Happiness on Three Levels

Happiness is an imaginary condition, formerly attributed by the living to the dead, now usually attributed by adults to children, and by children to adults.

—Thomas Szasz

My life has no purpose, no direction, no aim, no meaning, and yet I'm happy. I can't figure it out. What am I doing right?

—Charles Schulz

Let's think about developing ourselves in three stages. The first stage has to do with the self. This is the stage where we heal and get to know and accept ourselves. The second level is about healing our relationships with others. It is the stage of working with understanding, compassion, and eventually, service. The third stage, which is based on the clarity and healing from the first two levels, is about the expression of freedom and wisdom. Here we have reached the place of inner coherence where our actions become the natural expression of balance, harmony, and our inner sacred nature. We will talk about each stage in sequence, even though they appear in life in a more circular way.

Selfishness Is a Good Place to Start

We must begin here, in the present moment, where our breath and our body touch the earth in the here and now.

The foundation level of development is always the self. It is really most of the path. It is the physical, emotional, and energetic anchor that holds our awareness in this construct of reality that we call our life. It is the place where our ancestral patterns meet the bigger consciousness, all the while creating a biological container and conveyor that moves us through the illusion of time and space. To solve the riddle of the meaning of our physical incarnation and then master it, we must become fully part of the "real" world, while at the same time understanding it for what it is: an illusion that is both intricate and profound and is ours to refine and develop any way we choose.

If we accept the possibility of this other ephemeral reality, the direct experience of it becomes possible. In the early 1980s, I attended a ten-day Vipassana retreat led by a profound and insightful teacher named Goenka and his wife. There were about 150 of us there in a huge tent pitched in a field in northern California. The retreat was a very powerful experience for me, as it was the first time that I had undergone the intensity of twelve- to fourteen-hour days of meditation practice. In the evening of the seventh day, after the evening practice period, I went

We must begin here, in the present moment, where our breath and our body touch the earth in the here and now.

outside. The firm and stable reality of the world changed. I could see the space within the forms of the solid world around me. My body and the earth appeared translucent. I could see through my feet and the ground that they were standing on. Everything was formed of light and energy. This experience lasted until I fell asleep much later that evening.

In hindsight I can see that this experience shifted me as much as my "infinity" experience as a boy. I have never seen myself or the living world around me with the same eyes. As we begin to first become familiar with and then to "play" with reality, it becomes possible to hold them both in our consciousness. If I remember to include both realities in my mind as I go through my day, I can see the world while simultaneously seeing the energy and space within it. Everyone has the innate ability to experience wider and wider vistas of who we are. It's like a baby discovering that he is playing with his own foot—that it is connected to his own body. "What a revelation!"

Giving Ourselves Permission to Be a Little Selfish

The word "selfish" has bad connotations in our society. Truly selfish people are not considered in very high regard; they are the villains of our stories and cultural myths. But what is at the root of their behavior? If people are hungry, we feed them. If they are thirsty, we give them water. So if someone is hungry for love and attention and thirsty for acceptance and recognition, why do we find it so hard to feed them these nutrients that are just as vital to a decent life? But this is not the kind of selfishness I am talking about here. I'm talking about a healthy kind of selfishness—the kind that is not only good for us, but helps and clarifies our relationships with others.

After working with people for over forty years, I can say without hesitation that being a little selfish, in a good way, is the place for anyone who is not happy to start.

One of my clients is Sabrina, a bright, middle-aged college professor at a small East Coast school. She has worked for many years to be able to offer something meaningful to her students and the world. She is known and respected in her field and loved by her students and fellow faculty members. But she finds herself generally frustrated, unexcited with her work, and unable to willingly give the love and attention to her husband that he deserves. She has had swelling and sometimes achy ovaries and sensitive digestion for more than a year.

Sabrina and I began her phone session by having her focus on the somatic sensations in her ovaries. I asked her to take notice of any sensations that might be in her pelvis, and also any emotions that might arise in the process. As she did this, Sabrina began talking about some of the specific concerns she had in her life. All of a sudden I realized what her problem really was.

"You need to take time off!" I said. "You need to take a week or a month or a year by yourself. You need to go away until you really want to come back to your husband and your work. During that time you must only consider *your* needs and pay no attention to what anybody else in the entire universe wants. If you can't be away that long, at least take a week or ten days as a beginning, with the understanding that you will take more time for yourself as soon as possible. Please accept that you fully deserve this time and that it will benefit not only you, but your husband, your students, and anyone else who routinely comes in contact with you!"

There was a stunned pause on the other end of the phone line. Sabrina replied, "When I heard you say that, my whole body relaxed. Just hearing it makes me feel good. I know what you're saying is true."

"Take a breath into your ovaries now," I said. "How do they feel?"

"They don't ache anymore," she said. "I feel so good."

Clinically, it is very common that just hearing the truth of our situation begins the healing. We all instinctively know what we want and need. Most of the time when something is wrong with our body or life it is because we are not paying attention to the inner promptings that are continually trying to get our attention. With a little experimenting, we can learn to trust our body's instincts and demands. I will repeat it again because it is so important: When we are thirsty we must drink. When we are hungry we must eat. When we are lonely and need companionship or physical intimacy, we are getting these messages for a reason. When we start listening and cooperating with the messages, we will immediately become healthier and happier.

The voices of our bodies and our heads often take different sides. When we are in balance and tuned in, the head can supply reason, information, and add perspective, but the body is almost always the true unconflicted voice if we can just "drop in" enough to feel what it is trying to tell us. We so often use a detached cerebral perspective to protect us from things that we don't want to think about or deal with.

Our minds become filled with a cacophony of cascading, conflicting, and insistent voices and ideas that obscure the important information that our inherently healthy mind is continually offering.

Deep Happy Inner Practice

Notice the Underlying Reality

In most cases, giving is good. In the initial process of our healing it is useful to notice how we really feel about where we are or what we are doing. Notice how you are feeling as you say or do something. As you have a conversation, notice how the room or the area around you feels. Consider whether the meaning of your words matches the feeling that you feel in your body when you speak them. Try noticing things that you don't say, too. It is also very useful to notice who and where you feel most comfortable and free to be yourself. It is usually very interesting to discover the gap between our outer and inner selves.

The more we are resistant or even unable to deal with something, the stronger these mental buffers become. When we hear a voice, a phrase, or a story that is continually repeating in our heads, we must realize that this is never the truth. The truth is simple—it doesn't repeat itself in an unending barrage, but rather speaks to us in a gentle tone that has nothing to sell. The intense and incessant thoughts are buffers that intentionally keep us from whatever it is inside us that we are resistant to hear or know, feel, or deal with.

This process is a large part of what modern drug-focused psychiatry tries to remedy. These simple patterns that we creatively develop to protect ourselves from overwhelm and trauma sooner or later coalesce into what can erroneously be categorized as depression, anxiety, paranoia, and compulsion, to list only a few. These diagnostic words can sound so intimidating that we forget that they are *all* just shifts in our physiology. They seem amorphous and out of our control because of our disconnection—our loss of the "felt sense" that is the key to navigating and healing the vast majority of so called "psychiatric" illnesses. How can drugs that numb and disconnect us heal? How can being drugged help these emotional and functional imbalances that are based on survival by disconnection? The vast majority of what we call depression, anxiety, and basic mental illness can be treated and healed with physical methods like acupuncture, homeopathy, neurofeedback, herbal and nutritional supplements, diet, psychotherapy, and when possible, family support.

This is hardly a difficult concept to understand. But, when we become so preoccupied with our busy lives, it becomes surprisingly easy to dismiss important requests from the body, even though they are so fundamental to Deep Happy.

So many of our common physical maladies are the result of this—we're simply not listening to the urging of our bodies. Constipation, for example, usually falls into this category. There are two fundamental causes of this problem, and they are both the result of not listening to the body. The first is putting off the body's basic urge to just go to the bathroom. This is common for busy people who place their schedule ahead of their body's needs. Instead of assisting the body in getting rid of waste when it wants, they keep putting it off until finally the body stops giving the messages. The second most common cause of constipation is simply not drinking enough water. Again, dehydration is usually the cause of not listening to the body when it is trying to tell you something.

"Hey, buddy! You're thirsty! Drink something! Duh!"

Discovering ourselves begins with discovering our bodies and how wonderfully they continually communicate to us what we need and how we are doing. It's hard not to admit that being in our bodies is our most fundamental life predicament. It must be an important part of why we are here, because here we are, living in them.

Most of us have a lot of catching up to do. We often don't realize how many unexpressed thoughts and feelings are hiding in there. When we find ourselves lingering on the thought, idea, word, or phrase that somebody has just said, it is likely to be an indicator we are holding on to something inside us and reacting to it. Last night at dinner, I was talking to a friend, Michael, about this chapter and the idea of selfishness. He is an incredibly kind and intelligent person who, like many people, often puts the needs of others ahead of his own. When I mentioned the word "selfish," he immediately made a subtle face and went off on the idea that maybe selfishness was not a good thing. I knew he had heard me talk on this subject before, so I was surprised by his reaction. After few minutes, I realized that the word "selfish" had reminded him of something he felt I had been selfish about. This proved to be true. He had not wanted to bother me with something his head told him was trivial, but in fact had been more perturbed by it than he consciously knew. It turned out that I had promised to drive him somewhere while his car was getting fixed, but had canceled at the last minute because I had to pick up my son from school. This bubble of irritation had been swimming around inside of Michael without him realizing it for several weeks. How many times have we been hurt or angered by something that someone did or said yesterday, last week, last year, or when we were ten? That's how far behind we are. Those moments when we discover these multiple levels are such a gift. When we notice them and follow them in, interesting doors to all the unfinished and unhealed places inside of us open and give us the opportunity for house cleaning and reorganization. As we give ourselves permission and courage to explore these unfinished and often unutilized and important parts of ourselves, we gradually become coherent, and the chaos of our incessant inner experience unifies into simple recognition of what is really going on.

In this process we will also discover our instinctual self, the self-protective mechanism present in all biological systems. It mandates our safety and survival. These are well-honed programs buried in the oldest parts of our brain, nervous system, and primal consciousness. When we are walking in the woods and suddenly jump to the side after catching sight of a curved object on the ground, or instantly retract our finger from something hot, we are experiencing our primal protective abilities. There is no downside in jumping away from a curved stick—the great upside is that it might have been a snake. Our primal response bypasses the frontal cortex of the brain and goes straight to our motor system, which quickly stimulates the nerves and muscles to pull our hand away.

This instinctual part of us is buried deep and for the most part functions separately from our consciousness. But as the static of unreleased trauma builds up in our bodies and creates conflicting messages in our nervous system, the line between this primal or limbic part of our functioning and a normal reasoning, integrated self can become muddied and indistinct. This is why we sometimes respond with much greater intensity than a situation should normally call for. This condition is called PTSD, or post-traumatic stress disorder. In this situation, a part of our the brain called the hypothalamus, which is responsible for orienting us in time and space, becomes overshadowed by the chronically overstimulated amygdala, which is an emergency response part of the limbic, primitive, and emotionally aware brain. Since we have never released the trauma, part of us is always on ready alert, waiting to react instantly before we even realize what is happening. By simply watching and getting to see our selves with curiosity and not judgment, we will gradually be able to shift the over-reactivity to more appropriate expressions of who we are.

Giving and helping others nourishes our hearts and our humanness.

There is a very interesting paradox that shows itself when we focus on ourselves in a healthy way. The more we tune into our real selves, the more we seem to tune in to others and the even the world around us. We are wired to respond to and perceive the inner workings of other humans and even other life forms. We are also intimately connected and responsive to both the micro and macro influences of nature. The sounds of crickets, energies radiating from the sun, the movements of the stars, all touch us and have a direct influence on our lives. The more we let ourselves be us, the more in harmony with creation we become.

Giving and helping others nourishes our hearts and our humanness.

The Selfless Heart

I became aware of the condition of my emotional and spiritual heart in December 1980 when I first had my pulse taken in the way of Chinese medicine by Michael Broffman. He spent about ten minutes feeling the radial pulses of both wrists, and then proceeded to describe my life to me. His simple description of the traumas and difficulties at the ages at which they occurred immediately changed how I understood myself and clarified the steps that I needed take in my own healing and development.

We often don't realize how difficult or unusual our lives were when we were children. Of course sometimes we make things out to be worse than they were, but more often than not, we minimize the difficulties we endured, not realizing the lingering effects those early experiences had on the rest of our lives.

For me, being the only child of two dysfunctional families left me with a great deal of emotional pain, little familiarity with real intimacy, and no idea of what it was to live from my heart and feel safe and supported. It was always easy for me to be emotionally open to animals, strangers, and to a certain extent, friends. However, I was very inexperienced and uncomfortable when someone came too close to my heart. My saving grace was that somehow I understood my situation and that I needed to fix my shortcomings. For the first several years after leaving home, I created specific situations for myself that would require letting go of my old habits of protection and learning about family in group situations. These included living in several ashrams, a spiritual community, and a number of shared living situations.

After my pulse reading, I was even more diligent in learning to feel and live from my heart, though it took time for me to feel comfortable at it. I was thirty-one and had just left the acupuncture program that I had created at the Pacific College of Naturopathic Medicine. My life was open. I retreated to my house in the redwoods in Cazadero, California, lost the thirty-five pounds I had gained from stress in fifty days, and dug in to any part of me that I could find that was still unhealed. Through long hours of meditative practice and long distance running, I worked to notice any resistance or fear or closed places within me, letting go and relaxing into whatever situation I was in. I also diligently worked to uncover and heal my own heart using specific meditative and Qigong practices, sometimes spending hours going into the area of my heart-loosening any of the old habitual emotional and energetic holding patterns that I could find. There were terrifying moments of feeling latent hurt or of feeling so uncomfortable when another heart wanted to touch mine. I began to recognize the process by which I had learned to divert my attention or minimize my ability to feel emotionally. I also got used to not taking my thoughts and feelings quite so seriously.

One day during that period, I woke up to a mind full of crazy thoughts and feelings. The bigger part of me recognized the cascading chaos of my "inner symphonies of disturbance" for what they were: the release of pent-up historic material that had been pried loose from my body and subconscious that was floating to the surface to be released. I had patients scheduled in my clinic that day, so I decided to try an experiment. I took all the craziness in my head and just moved it way over to one side. It was like I put the TV on in the other room. I could still hear the crazy thoughts, but they didn't bother me. By the afternoon I noticed that that part of my mind was calm and coherent again, and I brought it back in to the central part of my awareness. After doing this a few times, I could see that the crazy inner dialogue was not the real me. It was just a bubble of stuck phenomena trying to get out.

Other days during that time, I woke up feeling terrible—emotionally and even physically unwell. I found that if I just selflessly gave everything I could to my patients, by the end of the day I felt good again. Since by then I was used to my patterns, it became less important for me to specifically focus on them. Instead I focused on giving and service, keeping a small awareness of the inner process.

Through this, my ability to love and give took on a spontaneous naturalness, which moved past the polite expectations of work and friendship. This opening worked in two directions. The first and most obvious was that I could give more fully without consideration for my own need—to put myself aside, as it were, and to fill the needs of my clients, friends, and family. I also gained the ability to recognize situations where giving became interfering and where it was more important to let people and situations work themselves out on their own.

To recognize when helping and service are too little or too much is a process of intuition, humility, and inner knowing and takes a lifetime to master.

Nothing Special—Everything Special

As we allow ourselves to be loved and nourished by the universe, letting the love and nourishment seep all the way into our marrow, our incessant need to have, to protect, or to convince falls away. Eventually our reactive needs dissolve into an "everyday nothing special" way of being. From there creative spontaneity, warmth, and unattached passion naturally arise.

Since at this stage we have mostly healed the self and the selfless—the part of us that gives completely—we can more fully trust our intuition and our inclinations. To the degree that we have weeded out the reactive or empty places within ourselves, our need for greed, power, dishonesty, cruelty, unconscious aggression, or any similar negative pattern virtually disappears. Like the samurai of medieval Japan, as we reach a level of healthy coherence, we become afraid neither to live nor to die. We are guided by our innate wisdom that arises each moment, as it is needed to help us act, assist, and just be.

In this way we can live in the everyday normality of miracles, where nothing is special and everything is special. Healthy passion and divine creativity merge with the increasingly unfettered experience of living our lives. Simplicity and purity of our intent becomes a powerful channel for the universe to express itself through us.

Working with Pain and Suffering

As we move from beginning to know how and who we are through our personal development, the quality of our suffering changes. When we are locked into our patterns, any startling invasion of our reality can be difficult and painful. The more we heal into coherence, the less we have to resist. Without resistance, there is no ledge for the pain or suffering to sit on.

Pain and suffering are also mitigated by perspective. If I have a tack in my foot and I focus on that foot, the pain seems very strong and I'm very uncomfortable. If my focus includes my leg and my foot with the tack sticking in it, it still hurts, but the sensation is watered down from the slightly bigger perspective. If I experience my whole body with the tack my foot, the pain seems even less. This gives us a lot of okay input and only a small amount of tack-in-my-foot input. If I notice the tack in my foot and also take in the whole world around me, I still have to get the tack out of my foot, but the experience of it will seem minor because I am also experiencing the rest of my life. The tack becomes just another bit of reality to handle.

To recognize when helping and service are too little or too much is a process of intuition, humility, and inner knowing.

When we are not happy, it is usually because our perspective is too small.

I have worked with thousands of people in all kinds of pain. As soon as we begin to actually describe what we are feeling, it is not uncommon for the quality of the sensation to change. This process also works with emotions. If we pay close enough attention to how and where our emotions feel in our body, they dissolve. Most people are surprised that emotions are actually physical manifestations in the body. When we combine this with keeping a larger view in focus, it becomes so much easier to not take things personally and to keep perspective. When working through difficult emotional issues with others, it is useful to remember that each of us is doing our best at each moment.

As a society we have been locked into the "eye-for-an-eye" reality, where punishment and retribution were looked to for solutions to social and personal problems, for far too long. We have all seen the effects of this less-than-perfect strategy. If we are really and truly to create an earth that nurtures and protects each living being, it is imperative that we learn to shift our social attitude to one of understanding and compassion. In that paradigm, benefit to the individual and the whole are seen as irrevocably intertwined. Once the world can make the shift to an ecology of the human heart that holds a unifying intent for life, then the basic structures of our global family will also change. Imagine the legal system that was based not on blame, but understanding each person's ability (or lack of it) to function in society. Where the remedy for problems was not punishment or incarceration, but rather based on a strategy for helping each person to grow and change. Of course there would be some who were unable to do this—who would need to be kept

When we are not happy, it is usually because our perspective is too small.

separate from society as a whole—but what if that separation included kindness and respect? Imagine an educational system where the children were clearly shown the effects of their actions, both positive and negative. Where in the process of learning the important subjects, they also learned to identify and use their inner guidance to know right from wrong and how they really felt about things.

To the degree that we are able heal the traumas and disconnected places within each of us, the world and civilization can heal.

Imagine a scientific ethic that was guided by curiosity in its purest form—one that was not limited by ideas of what was and was not scientific—one that kept the larger implications of new discoveries and research without the manipulating and corrupting effects of financial interests.

And finally, imagine a health care system that understood the innate intelligence of the body and the disease process and was based on allowing the intelligence of the body to express and heal itself.

In spite of our failings, humanity has created wonders and miracles. As we honestly face the depth and difficulty of our world's situation, we can and will find solutions. But we must be open minded about what these solutions might demand of us in terms of our personal lifestyles and social structure. It is always useful to be reminded of something Albert Einstein once said: "Solutions cannot be created using the same mentality that created the problem."

To the degree that we are able heal the traumas and disconnected places within each of us, the world and civilization can heal.

5

The Art of the Heart

Our job is not to look for love; our job is to find all the places within us that resist it and love them.

—Rumi

Of all the topics I could talk about in this book, there is none more important than the heart. The heart is the foundation for Deep Happy—it is the organ of happiness! Of course I am talking about more than just the organ itself—I am talking about the heart as an emotional, energetic, and spiritual center.

When we hold a loved one close to us, or hug a small kitten or puppy to our chest, we have the ability feel the tactile sensation of love and tenderness right in our chest. We all know this, though many of us shut off the feelings in our hearts long ago. It is no wonder that heart disease is so prevalent, especially among women who have traditionally worn the mantle of feeling and compassion. I am not sure that it is still common knowledge that we can use our hearts for guidance and wisdom. Just noticing how our hearts feel at any given moment when we are trying to make a decision can tell us if we are on the right track. Most of us are unaware of how much we hold numbness and hurt in our chests, so it may take a little time to feel and know our hearts again.

Deep Happy Inner Practice

Connecting to the Heart

Relax for a moment and gently take a few breaths into your heart area. Does it feel warm, open, and alive, or numb and tight? Maybe you don't feel much of anything. Please don't worry if that is the case; it's just tension from stress. If you begin to feel and breathe into your heart area, it will begin to open. Sometimes when this happens, we might feel an emotion, or even laugh or cry. These are good things—enjoy them. The heart can heal. You have just begun the process.

In my own life, uncovering and discovering the deep nature of my own heart has been seminal to my personal development. I have already written about my emotional difficulties with my families. I learned to doubt myself and to either shut off or not trust my feelings. I carried deep emotional pain that kept me from trusting or knowing my deeper heart.

One day in college, I met three different girls. Back home, I couldn't decide who to ask out. It didn't occur to me to notice which one I felt comfortable with, or if any of them touched my heart. I was totally in my head. This is a common thing in our culture. In my practice, I use the technique of Chinese pulse diagnosis that I described in an earlier chapter to also look at the bonding experiences my clients have with each of their parents. From this I can assess the emotional habits that have been passed along. If one or both parents was absent, controlling, emotionally closed, passive aggressive, and so forth, it is imprinted in us and forms a foundational style and tone that shades everything we do. These influences are not all bad—they create many interesting differences in personality and form the basis upon which our life's karmic work is laid out for us. The problematic parts can be healed, and the beneficial aspects can be enhanced or enjoyed.

The perception of a loving attitude has many disguises.

"My father loved me!" I often hear in tone that fully expresses a head-love rather than a heart-love. Almost always after a few moments of considering what I am describing, these clients remember the whole picture of their relationship with their parents. When we have a clear idea of where we have been, it's much easier for us to move forward. In abusive families the qualities of anger, castigation, and even corporal punishment can often be construed as love to young children and even subservient spouses. These inflictions are carried until they are released by personal healing processes like Deep Happy, various kinds of transformational therapies, the experiences of life, or the passing of the body. Though many wisdom traditions teach that these wounds and tendencies are carried until we can finally face them.

When we talk about someone, the tone of our voice always expresses the tone of whatever our relationship with them has been. In his own way, that father did love his daughter or son. However, due to his own emotional baggage he was unable to express this love from the feeling center of the heart in his chest. Love from the heart center is unconditional. It feels nourishing and freeing and loving. Love from the head involves emotional separation and often has rules and judgments; it doesn't feel safe or validate us for who we are, which is the most important nourishment that any of us can receive as we develop.

The feeling tone of the heart is very powerful. Most of us have felt it. Let me give you a wonderful if not unusual example.

In the early 1980s, I opened up a small office just off the town square in Sonoma, California. It was a small office with a waiting room in the front and a treatment room in the back. Because I was just starting my practice in that town and had little money, I slept on the couch in the waiting room each night.

I had gotten the office from a friend who was leaving town on the condition that I feed the small group of rabbits that lived in the central backyard that all the houses and buildings on the block shared. Apparently they had been pets of several ex-residents and had been let go, and for some strange reason they liked birdseed. So each morning I woke up early, and in my bathrobe and rubber boots I would go out to feed the bunnies.

There were six or seven rabbits in the group, led by little black female. For the first few weeks they wouldn't come near me. They stayed perhaps forty or fifty feet away, regarding me with great curiosity and waiting for me to sprinkle the seeds on the ground. After I'd moved back, they would come over to munch on their breakfast. One morning, without really thinking about it, I kneeled down and sent a beam from my heart to the heart of the little black female. I had never done anything like that before—it just happened. I swear I could see the beam of energy traveling across the yard. At the exact second that the beam from my heart touched the heart of this little black rabbit, she sat up straight, looked right at me, ran over to where I was, and nuzzled me. The other little rabbits followed her, and from that day on I could touch and pet all of them. It all seemed quite normal at the time, but in hindsight it was a moment that highlighted the work that I would do for the rest of my life, both with myself and with those who come to me for help. In Chinese medicine, the heart is seen as the center of the body and consciousness. Modern research in the new field of neurocardiology, sponsored by Heart Math (a private research and educational institute dedicated to heart research) and other sources, supports the ancient Chinese view. There is now a huge amount of scientific data supporting the heart's central function.

Heart Facts

I'll list a few of the remarkable scientific facts about the heart.

Our hearts beat one hundred thousand times a day, forty million times a year, and three billion times in a lifetime.

Embryologically, the heart begins to beat before the brain is even formed. Five days after a woman misses her period, there is a head-of-a-pin-sized heart pumping single red cells. Later comes the motor responsive, the emotional, and finally the intellectual brain. All major spiritual traditions use the heart as a focus for development. The electrical field of the heart is five thousand times greater than the brain. The heart's influence on the brain is greater than the brain's influence on the heart. As much as 85 percent of the heart's cells have embedded neurological or glial cells.

Heart cells, in vitro, beat together. Incoherence in the heart's rhythm clouds thinking and cognitive ability. Connecting to our heart switches us from our sympathetic to our parasympathetic or integrated part of our nervous system. The heart, when it beats, communicates with the entire body through nerve impulses, hormones, neurotransmitters, and pressure waves.

Considered from an esoteric or spiritual point of view, embryologically the heart descends from the top of the developing head, just below the crown chakra. The heart can connect this to the higher octave of awareness, and forms the basis of our deeper spiritual development. Gradually, as we become accustomed to higher and higher spiritual vibrations, the heart transmits the tone and frequency of our spiritual connection throughout the body, and as we go through daily life this tone and feeling gets transmitted into the world.

We have all felt someone's heart. We have all seen or come in contact with someone with whom we felt love and compassion right away. When we are inspired we can feel the radiance of our own hearts propelling us to fulfill our destiny.

Most cultures have sayings like "the heart of the matter" or "working with heart." We understand that love and kindness are the quintessential foundation of any healthy society. We even have a holiday dedicated to the heart, Valentine's Day, though the deeper meaning of the day is often overlooked. Is is not a surprise that heart disease is such a common illness in our society, yet when the causes of heart disease are detailed, an emotionally closed heart rarely makes the list.

In an enlightened health care system, all diagnosis would consider the symptoms of:

Slight thoracic tension

Facial tension

Stiffness at the upper mid-back

Coldness at the nape of the neck

Food allergies and gastrointestinal problems

Diabetes and autoimmune diseases

Sarcastic attitude

Pervasive fear or doubt

Tendency to settle for less

Hints of frustration or anger in the voice or a monotone voice

Accentuated intellectualism

Lack of intuition

and *many, many* other little indications as signs of this deeper energetic heart pathology.

When working with someone in opening their heart, it is common that they express concern. Often they feel that it is unsafe to open themselves emotionally. This is the greatest misunderstanding about the heart. In Chinese medicine and other systems, there are many emotional styles of defense. One style would be creating a wall of density or hyperactivity between the world and ourselves; other examples would be emotionally slipping away and avoiding agreement; or spacing out and disconnecting. Each of these styles relates to specific organ imbalances-—liver, spleen, pericardium, and so forth. When given free rein, the heart uses a very unique style of defense—it protects itself with openness. The heart feels safest when there is complete openness to the world. Things are seen and understood as they are. Difficulties can be anticipated and challenges prepared for. The quality that makes the openness of the heart safe is courage. Being willing to face reality is both the optimal quality of the heart and a process that strengthens and heals the heart.

The Chinese character for awakening or enlightenment, "Wu," depicts a heart, the number five, and a door—in other words, a heart with five open senses.

Let the gentle heart to be open and aware . . .

Listening, seeing, sensations, thoughts, people experiences, never wavering

Resting in the essence of its own true nature . . .

The connection of the heart to spiritual practice and development is extremely important. In a lifetime of researching spirituality, I have finally learned to pay very close attention to the quality of "heart." When I'm presented with a teacher or system, I always notice if I can feel the heart in the teacher's voice or essence or if the system emphasizes the heart. Being in the heart does not mean being weak and vulnerable. It means being strong and connected to who we are, what feels right, and what is important.

Just now, as I was writing this, my dog Trevor walked over and leaned against me. This is his way of saying, "Hello, I love you." He was the runt of the litter and as a result of his early experience he was a little distant when he first came to live with us. For the last two years we have loved him with all our hearts. He can now love and be loved. You can see it in his eyes and feel it when you are near him. He loves all other animals, especially our cat, who frequently has to put up with being licked. In the same way, you can feel the presence of heart in a teacher or a book. We all have the ability to recognize love. It has a specific feel and tone that makes us feel like we're home again. Some are so traumatized that they can only feel mistrust or even fear in the presence of love.

Judgment

Judgment is a real cancer in our society. The opposite of love, it signals that the heart is not involved. The process of the heart does involve discrimination, but in the sense of seeing and perceiving the widest truth of a situation. This is quite different from what I am calling judgment. When we remember that the true nature of each of us is equally part of a living universe, and that each of us has the same sacred essence, we are remembering the truth of the heart. When we can hold this reality of the heart in regard to each other, we can see that the aberrant traits of personality and lifestyle are just external elements due to past imprinting.

This does not mean that we have to let someone into our life or our home whom we don't like or don't feel good around. It means that first we must see the sacred being inside them surrounded by the difficulties of their personality. Secondly it means that we examine the parts of ourselves that seem reactive to that person. When we are annoyed or bothered by someone, it is because something inside us is triggered by them. If we learn to pay close attention to not just our feelings, but to the places in our body where we feel them, we can learn to let them go and change the physical patterns that hold them.

Research has shown that negative attitudes and expectations greatly limit the ability of children to love themselves and function well in society. In the same way, our unconscious negative attitudes toward anyone who is not healed can keep that person from growing and changing. The worst example of this is in our prison population. In no way do I advocate letting those who are unable to keep from negatively impacting society go free until and if they're able to handle themselves. But our societal judgment against their intrinsic worth keeps them from adopting the behaviors that we blame them for not having. This is both inhumane and nuts.

Another example of this is how we treat smokers. We have turned them into pariahs, yet all they are doing is trying to handle their stress. By making them feel so bad about smoking, we are making it even harder for them to quit. If you've ever taken a puff of a cigarette when you were stressed, you know that cigarettes work well, in the short term, for making you feel better and less stressed. In Chinese medicine guilt is an emotion that negatively impacts the lungs. In my opinion, the guilt and stress we put on smokers makes it more likely that they will suffer from lung disease and cancer. Instead of shaming them, it seems obvious to me that kindly supporting them and helping them to find ways to handle their stress and challenges would be a better solution. Loving them anyway is the best way to help them.

Deep Happy Inner Practice

Working with Our Judgment

Think about the little judgments you carry with you. The ones that are a part of your normal way of seeing others—how you also see and judge yourself.

Notice how these "judgments" keep you separated from others, keep you from really understanding their situation. Think of ways to let go of these. How would it feel to accept others just as they are? Yourself? Over time, notice subtler and subtler forms of judgment. Forgive yourself for not being perfect.

Forgiveness

Forgiveness is also directly related to the heart. Forgiving someone does not mean that whatever they did was okay. It means holding the truth of the inner sacred essence of each person, while at the same time seeing their ability or inability to express that essence in their life. Forgiveness does at least two things. It allows us to move on, which is usually a very good basis for the rest of our life. When we hold feelings and ideas of blame and revenge, we poison ourselves. When we forgive, there is a much greater likelihood that those who have wronged us can have the opportunity to reflect and change. Keeping the situation polarized with our anger, blame, or sense of victimization is not good sense, let alone wisdom. Of course there are times when the anger and outrage can be strong proponents for change and even necessary revolution, but this is a moving, creative energy that is not the same as blame and rage.

There are those who will neither reflect nor change. A friend of mine, a woman psychiatrist, works in San Quentin, a prison in Marin County, California. She says that about 85 percent of the prisoners she works with are able to change and heal, if given the proper time and attention. The other 15 percent, she says, are so traumatized that there is not much you can do with them. This 15 percent probably belong where they are, though hopefully within a more enlightened and humane system.

In the 1970s, while studying acupuncture in Boston, I worked in a lockup facility with delinquent teenage boys. They were all bigger and smarter than I was. They had learned to survive in the world through intimidation and manipulation, and they were very good at it. Growing up in the suburbs, I had very little experience with that kind of seething street aggression. I also didn't have the self-confidence to trust my intuition and instincts. Imagine taking those boys and adding years in prison with increasing disconnection from society and no supportive family or anything to hope for all. I think you can imagine what the 15 percent that were untouchable in prison might be like.

The challenge is to face the uncomfortable feelings that people who are different from us will sometimes make us feel. Again, I certainly do not advocate allowing sociopathic personalities to run freely in society, but if we can remember that they're human beings with hearts and souls, no matter how buried, then perhaps we can remember to love them while clearly seeing their inability to express their humanity because of their traumas and conditioning.

When we remember that time and space are relative and that our consciousness is vast and creative and simultaneously exists in many realities, it may be easier to understand that each of our lives has meaning no matter what the outer circumstances may be. By remembering to love the unlovable, we plant seeds for other times and places. Again, this does not mean that we love their actions or condone them; it just means that we honor the essence of their deep being while being vitally aware of the painful expression held in the personality.

Surprising things are possible, though. In 1971 I had a job taking care of pre-delinquent boys outside of Portland, Oregon. They were aged nine to fourteen, and most of their families were either dead or in jail. They had all committed crimes. One nine-year-old had robbed a bank with a .45 automatic that he could hardly hold in two hands. Most of them were still little boys and had not completely cut themselves off emotionally.

I started working there in the fall. The facility was surrounded by open land; just beyond where the lawn ended there were large fields of high grass full of snakes. The boys were always testing new staff. Sitting in the chair in the living room one day during my first week, I was suddenly confronted with two boys standing in front of me. Each had three or four snakes in both hands. I have always liked looking at snakes, but have never been comfortable handling them. Fortunately, I recognized what they were doing soon enough to force a smile and to pretend with all my might that I was excited and happy to see these squirming snakes wriggling inches from my face. I reached out and lightly patted a couple snakes, muttering something like, "cool snakes" and wondering if my sphincters would ever relax. Such was my first week there.

During my introductory interview for that job, I was told to be aware of the small boy named John, the bank robber, who was considered sociopathic—unable to form real relationships—and was highly manipulative. During my first few weeks there, John was always kind and friendly, making positive comments about my clothes or my new haircut. I began to doubt his diagnosis—"He's such a nice boy, they must be wrong." I woke up from that overly optimistic view when I overheard a conversation John was having in his room with several of the boys.

"I think we got this new guy Peter all buttered up now."

I suddenly realized how smart and crafty this little nine-year-old was.

Several weeks after that, it was my turn to help John clean up after our evening meal. After the other boys left the dining room, we began to carry the dishes into the kitchen. He suddenly dropped to the kitchen floor, sitting cross-legged with his arms folded defiantly across his chest. He said,

"You can kick me, beat me, hit me. I don't care, I am not doing the dishes!"

At first I had no idea what would be the best course of action. I guess divine intervention happened, because without any idea what I was doing, I started to sing and dance around him.

My stepmother loved Frank Sinatra. For years Frank Sinatra was always playing in the background at our house—it was the soundtrack for that dysfunctional part of my childhood. When I die and my life passes before my eyes the soundtrack will most certainly be Frank Sinatra. So of course the song that I sang while ridiculously dancing around little John as he sat defiantly on the floor was a Sinatra tune.

You make me feel so young,
you make me feel like spring has sprung,
and every time I see you grin,
I'm such a happy individual . . .

I sang all three verses in pure spontaneity, without the slightest idea of what I was doing. During all this, John just looked up at me with the funniest look on his face, tilting his head occasionally like a confused puppy. When I finished, John stood up, put a hand on each of my shoulders, and gently butted his head into my heart. Then we went and did the dishes together, both of us not saying much. It was the first and last time that anyone knew of when John had expressed tenderness and emotion.

I have thought about that incident many times over the years. I believe that what caused my moment with John was the out-of-the-blueness of it all. There was no judgment or intent, just a moment of lightness and fun that cut through the mechanism of disconnection where John had learned to hide all of his troubled life. Through grace, we were able to enter a neutral space beyond the histories that colored who we both were. In succeeding weeks, I unsuccessfully tried to duplicate the experience, but it was never the same. John's defensive mechanism was now alert to that sort of thing.

Writing this forty years later, I understand that this was another one of the important lessons in my life. Building on that experience, I have worked to be able to return to that essential place of neutrality and humanity and have found that miracles can happen there. It is truly the domain of the heart, beyond judgment and forgiveness.

The idea of forgiveness brings up several common reactions. The most common reaction I get from clients or participants in my seminars is, "Oh, I've already forgiven everyone. None of it matters to me anymore." And for the most part, this is true—at least as far as their conceptual understanding goes. But it is normal for the head and body to be in great disagreement on this point.

Just the other day, I was working with a client of mine, Andrew, who said that he had worked out all his frustration about his father. He said he had forgiven him, and that was that. Through pulse diagnosis and his tone of voice I could tell that Andrew's father had been quite angry and abusive with him. As I began to gently question him about his father, his jaw began to tighten and his voice carried much less warmth and resonance. His breathing got shallower and his lower abdomen contracted. As I pointed this out to him, at first he was a bit defensive; then he realized the truth of it and was surprised at how much emotion and anger he still had for his father. Once we realize how much of our body's reactions are held in, there is a straightforward process to work it out—it just takes a little time. For forgiveness to be real it must be with our whole heart, body, and mind. Even a little of one is better than nothing, but eventually it is useful to clear all that we can.

A friend of mine, Hank, used to do therapy with an E-Meter. This is a device used by Scientologists. Hank was not a Scientologist, but he used one anyway. An E-Meter is a very sensitive device—a GSR or Galvanic Skin Response biofeedback device. It measures very subtle levels of arousal or anxiety in the nervous system. The therapist questions the client with various topics until the needle on the device moves, indicating suppressed or unfinished emotional or energetic experience. A seasoned therapist can quickly go deeper, finding little knots of unfinished history and feeling.

During this process I learned to forgive someone or change my feelings about a situation while at the same time understanding the deeper truth of it. If I forgave someone to the point where the E-Meter would show no more reactivity, inevitably the next time I saw the person in question, their outward response to me would be much friendlier and more open, even before I had a chance to say anything to them. Sometimes when I had cleared something with someone this way, I received a call from him or her even before I got home from the session. Through this process it became evident to me that as we change, the world around us changes.

Deep Happy Inner Practice

Forgiveness

Think of a person or situation that you have had trouble forgiving. First feel your own heart. Breathe into your chest. Remember with tenderness those whom you love. Now think of the person or thing that you have held in blame. This forgiveness is not about what they did to you or what you did—it is about recognizing that the cause was ultimately the internal pain and personal inner suffering that locks each of us away from own our heart, from our connection to others, and from the trust that we will have the life lessons we need.

Next, notice what thoughts or feelings still stand in the way.

Go back and forth with this process until there is nothing in the way.

Gratitude

Christine Carter, sociologist and happiness researcher at UC Berkeley, has found that gratitude is one of the most important foundations for happiness. In her research she has seen that those who have gratitude or learned to have gratitude experienced greater levels of happiness, health, and a great deal more meaning in their lives.

Gratefulness Practice

Stop and relax for a moment. Notice how your body feels. Relax again.

Take gentle, slow, deep breaths down into your lower abdomen.

Let the feeling of calmness and connection from the breathing flow through you.

Let yourself feel grateful—for your life, your health, the sunlight, your family, your dog, the clouds in the sky, the rain, or whatever touches you.

Let the feeling of gratefulness wash through your body as a physical sensation.

As you do this, notice any places in your body that resist this warm, soft feeling of gratefulness.

With a little practice, you can let the feelings and sensations of gratefulness gently dissolve into all the tight and closed places.

In time, you'll be able to fill every cell with gratefulness.

Carry this feeling with you throughout the day so it can change the whole tone and frequency of your body and your life. You might be surprised at how quickly things will start happening.

When life is going well, being grateful can be a natural response. How often do we get so absorbed in the "me-ness" of living, thinking that all that we have is the result of our physical efforts? This limitation is not just in the physical world but in confining our receptivity to the lessons, perspective, information, and wisdom that the universe is presenting to us every moment. The very act of being grateful opens the two-way exchange, allowing important and even unexpected possibilities to show up in our lives.

But how often do we really stop and feel grateful? Have you felt thankful or grateful today? Have you ever felt deep and sacred gratitude for all that has been given to you? If you can, stop reading this for a moment and let a feeling of being grateful soak into you. How does it feel? Imagine living with this feeling. You can. It just takes a little practice and remembering. You can use this basic practice of gratitude to heal yourself and your relationships.

Of course it's easy to be grateful when things are going well, but when things are difficult and challenging, it's normal to ask, "What do I have to be thankful for?" In cataclysmic moments like war, death, great illness, or financial distress, finding a moment of gratitude is usually the last thing on our minds. But when the tide turns, and we have a moment to breathe again, perhaps there will be small things that we can appreciate—maybe just that today is not as bad as yesterday. The more we are grateful for the little things, the better life becomes. An attitude of thankfulness allows us to recognize the benefits and opportunities that come to us each moment.

When we hone the subtlety of our perceptive ability enough, each moment lived becomes a lifetime in and of itself to be grateful for.

When we hone the subtlety of our perceptive ability enough, each moment lived becomes a lifetime in and of itself to be grateful for.

In the most difficult and trying times, we can still find the moments that are neither painful nor difficult. These moments-in-between can sustain us though other times that challenge us to our core. One surprising result of this outlook is that we learn to face and live through tragedy and challenge moment by moment. The thing that makes the most difficult times even worse is our fear and expectation of what might come. We can get used to being in the moment, not flinching from the truth of whatever appears in front of us.

The more we face our life, the easier it becomes and the better things seem.

In martial arts, this is called "investing in loss." If I am training as a fighter, the last thing I want to do is to be afraid of being hit. I want to be able to see the punch coming without hesitating or wincing. If I can unflinchingly see the punch coming directly at my face, time will slow down and I can make subtle shifts and respond in a way that fully utilizes my own power and creativity.

The more we face our life, the easier it becomes and the better things seem.

6

Asking for What You Want, Then Letting It In

All those who believe in telekinesis, raise my hand.

—Steven Wright

ASKING FOR WHAT WE want is important if we are to heal. It would seem like a simple thing, but so many of us are brought up to edit or limit what we ask for and how we ask for it. Last week I called one of my clients to see if I could switch her appointment time. Her words said, "Sure, no problem."

But the tone of her voice said, "That is not very convenient for me."

I was in a hurry and did not pay close enough attention to this detail and let it go. By the time our phone session came up, I had remembered the tone of her voice, and mentioned this to her.

"You know you can ask for what you want and tell me the truth," I said.

"Are you sure? You don't know what you're asking for!"

"Yes, I do," I replied, smiling to myself.

She laughed a little uneasily and mentioned that she was only kidding, but of course she really wasn't. She's a lovely woman of Korean descent from a successful and highly educated family. She was under the weight of both the female tradition of being submissive and the strict Asian tradition of being excessively polite. As we talked about this, she realized how difficult it was for her, in many instances, to really ask for what she wanted.

Deep Happy Inner Practice

Four Steps in Asking

1. First we become more and more honest about what it is that we think we want.
2. Then we notice how we feel about wanting it.
3. Then we notice how we feel about asking for it.
4. Finally, we practice and become adept at asking for exactly whatever it is.

Note: if it is really inappropriate to ask for something in a specific situation, please notice how you feel about not asking. Be alert to a better opportunity that might arise.

We won't always get what we want, but the process of first knowing and then acting frees us from the limitations of minimizing or ignoring our needs. This process will require skill and practice. For instance, we might not want to ask for something from our boss during a very busy or stressful time. Knowing and recognizing the needs of those we are asking will bring us awareness of the best way and time to implement them.

Things work very much the same on the micro level, where each cell and organ must communicate to the whole exactly what their needs are. Air, water, food, awareness of danger, removal of toxins, balance, and interaction are all critical to each cell and every system. But those are just the basic needs. Once we get beyond the basics that keep us alive, the needs of higher organisms become more complex and extend into the areas of love, respect, safety, connection, physical intimacy, and even personal satisfaction. These requirements are as important for our well-being as oxygen.

My own early years left me with deep-seated doubts about my worth and value as a person. My personality was fundamentally outgoing, but I was often unable to be that way because of the conflicted feelings I was holding inside. I didn't know how to ask for nourishment for my heart or help for the hurt that was buried deep within me. When I had brushes with the love or healthy attention I so needed, I didn't know how to accept it, physically or emotionally. As the years passed and I began to understand what was possible, I found that the more I trusted who I was and asked for just what I wanted, the happier I became. When I was fourteen, I spent lots of time at the local pool during the summer. Most days I would ride my bike over with friends and swim in the highly chlorinated water. There were lots of other kids floating and splashing, surrounded around the pool's edge by mothers chatting on the lounge chairs pretending not to be drinking martinis out of their thermoses. It was the early 1960s, and the movie and TV star Troy Donahue was all the rage in surf movies, with his combed-back blond hair with the big wave in front. I wanted girls to like me, and thought they would if I looked like Troy Donahue.

One day after swimming I was combing my hair in the club's locker room, gazing at myself in the mirror as only a fourteen-year-old can do and noticing how blond my chlorinated hair had become in the sun. There must have been a lot of extra chlorine in the pool, judging from the amount of it that was dried in my hair. As I combed it, the chlorine made it stick together in just a certain way, and as I saw it in the mirror, superbly captured by the ceiling light perfectly placed above me, I realized that I had reached a "Troy Donahue hair perfection moment." My life held new meaning and possibility. I prayed:

"Please God, may my hair never change, may it always stay just like this!"

Looking back on that moment, I am eternally thankful that what I asked for was blatantly and completely ignored by the great intelligence of this universe, who at that very moment was offering more love and compassion than I could understand by not granting my prayer. If indeed I had gotten my wish that chlorinated afternoon in suburban Michigan, it's probably fair to speculate that I might not be here today writing this. Who knows? I might have been sucked in to a very different cultural milieu, perhaps with other relationship and job opportunities more in sync with my pompadour and chlorinated blond hair.

For this I am greatly and humbly appreciative!

Letting It In

The other aspect of allowing and getting nourishment is letting it in. Dry sponges don't absorb water right away—it takes them a few moments to gradually let the moisture be absorbed. If we have been emotionally dry and protected, it may be scary to think about being open and receptive. A perfect example of this process is our own digestive system, whose job it is to let us know by smell, taste, and memory if we should eat something or pass it by.

In Asian medical systems, the digestive system represents the present time. For the GI system to be able to do its job, it must sense things in the moment so it can pass the information to our brain. If we smell or even just imagine corned beef hash, we get either an *ughhh* or an *ahh* feeling in our gut, letting us know that we should or shouldn't eat it. This same function also tells us if any other kind of situation is or isn't good. It could be anything—a possible new relationship, buying a car. We often override these simple messages, but as we get used to listening to them, life gets much easier.

The digestive system has another way of giving us subtle signals. Stomach problems are quite common in our modern lives, and most digestive and stress-related symptoms stem from pushing away the messages of worry that we are feeling in our gut. The more that we actually let ourselves feel the sensations there, the more quickly they will dissipate, as surprising as that may seem.

Of course wonderful and fulfilling experiences can nourish and uplift us, but are we always able to fully absorb their full potential? The last time you held someone you cared for, did you let the feelings in both of your hearts connect? Think of the last beautiful sunset you saw. How long did you linger with the sight of it? Were you able to take the essence and vibration of the colors inside of you, letting them shift the very tone of your nervous and hormonal systems? Did the moment change you in a profound way, even for a short time? Could you carry the sight or feeling of it with you during your day?

Let us remember to take all good things inside of us until there is no more room. Wherever we go then, peaceful and loving energy will spill out, infecting all we meet.

Why are we so resistant to the deeper experience of each moment? This is a question asked by poets, thinkers, and the great philosophers of our world. I believe that the answer is no more complicated than that we are just not used to doing it and don't know or remember how good it might feel.

Let us remember to take all good things inside of us until there is no more room. Wherever we go then, peaceful and loving energy will spill out, infecting all we meet.

Deep Happy Inner Practice

Letting Things In

Relax and breathe into your lower abdomen. Let your mind be calm and free. Take a few moments to really "sink in." Begin to think about something that you have sincerely wanted but have not yet been able to manifest. You could also think of a new direction that you would like your life to move into.

Feel your body as a totality of physical, energetic, and emotional sensations.

When you can feel yourself as a whole being, again think of what it is that you want.

Was there any tightening anywhere?

Could you feel your body, energy, or emotional self resisting letting in whatever you were thinking of?

Again, feel the totality of your felt self and gradually let yourself open in any of the places that you just felt tighten up.

Just keep relaxing and opening.

See what happens.

You have just opened your receptivity to the things you have wanted.

7

Suffering Is Optional

Life is full of misery, loneliness, and suffering—and it's all over much too soon.

—Woody Allen

It is by suffering that human beings become angels.

—Victor Hugo

Tell your heart that the fear of suffering is worse than the suffering itself. And no heart has ever suffered when it goes in search of its dream.

—Paulo Coelho

Pain and Body Sensations

Some of the greatest obstacles to happiness are physical and emotional pain. Until we have practiced Deep Happy or some other liberating method, it is hard not to feel the intrusion of difficult sensations in our body or psyche. Our friends, family, and society give us tacit permission to be unhappy when we are troubled or in pain. Pain is often seen as something intractable that we have to live with. Our current health care system is not especially good at identifying or in turn healing the deeper causes of pain. Care is usually based on enabling pain and illness because it takes the view that pain, disease, and illness are separate agents that attack us, instead of focusing on possible causes that are intimately linked to who we have become and what we are going through in our lives. Heaven forbid that there might even be an intelligence to illness or pain.

The word "pain" has very little actual meaning. It is usually used to indicate that there is some kind of unfamiliar or unpleasant sensation in an approximate area in the body or head. Yet when we begin to actually pay attention to the exact sensations we are experiencing, we find that what we called "pain" is a much more complex and detailed set of sensations and locations.

I usually suggest to my clients that rather than use the word *pain*, they instead describe the specific sensations that they feel and the exact location where they feel them. A few of the words that express these somatic sensations are numb, achy, hot, cold, throbbing, dull, sharp, electric, and so forth. I also suggest that they pay close attention to the location, shape, thickness, and even color and sound of what they are feeling. This kind of sensory focus may take a little practice. Even people with experience in meditation and mindfulness practice are often not used to noticing small and seemingly trivial shifts in small body areas. Using the breath in this process is very helpful.

Not feeling anything in a particular area is also a sensation. The lack of any perceptible feeling indicates a disassociation from that part of the body and usually indicates an area with held traumatic or emotional material. People who have been in pain for a long time often pay little attention to any variations in these sensations.

At our clinic we often ask just-treated patients how they're feeling and they say, "Oh, it always hurts."

"Yes, but how does it feel now?" I will ask.

"Oh, it always feels the same."

It may take a lot of prodding to get them to actually feel what sensations they're experiencing. Sometimes things even feel worse for a short while before they get better. As healing releases physical toxins and emotional residues, it is not unusual for patients to feel temporary joint pain, nausea, or even a slight headache. We know these are signs of healing because they last a short time and when they pass we feel better than we did before.

The more we actually feel the sensations within the pain, the less it hurts. The less we feel them, the more it hurts.

The almost universal response to paying closer attention to subtle sensations of the body is that what was previously felt as "pain" changes into an experience that is more understandable and manageable. It also returns a sense of personal control. More often than not, as we perceive the "pain" with increasing awareness, the pain begins to dissolve.

The more we actually feel the sensations within the pain, the less it hurts. The less we feel them, the more it hurts.

In the early 1970s I was working as a biofeedback therapist in the Los Angeles area. A wonderful psychiatrist named Mel Werebach had trained me. Mel was tall and well-dressed with shiny black hair and a close-cropped

Deep Happy Inner Practice

Dissolving Pain

Working with pain is much easier than it may sound. Begin this practice by doing some low abdominal breathing and relaxing your thoughts and body.

The first step in this process is to choose an area to work on—perhaps a back pain, headache, shoulder, or stomach pain. (Note: Most leg and lower extremity pain actually comes from the low back area, even if you have no pain there.) After relaxing, begin to focus your in and out breath in that area. If your mind starts to notice other areas, bring your attention back to the original focus.

What sensations do you feel there? Please use specific words to describe what you feel—achy, cold, numb, sharp, dull and so forth. Do not try to change any sensation—just do your best to feel it as clearly as you can. Usually the process of our awareness begins to open and move things. Be continually aware of how the sensations may be changing, either in the way that they feel, their movement, or even their depth and shape. Do not force this process. Just explore the sensations with interest and openness.

This process also works with emotional pain.

beard. His dark eyes were both interested and humorous. His view of science and reality was unfettered by academic or scientific prejudice. I had gotten a job at the UCLA Pain Control Unit in an attempt to learn acupuncture. While there, Mel and I struck up a friendship. He was very creative and open-minded, and we connected through impassioned conversations on a broad range of topics.

At that time I had some experience in meditation, energy healing and bodywork, and a little acupuncture. I was only just beginning to go deeper into the Western sciences. I had a strong basic understanding of how unexpressed emotional patterns and trauma are held in the body. Apparently Mel saw something in me and gave me an opportunity that I now know, with almost forty years of hindsight, was one of the most important experiences for shaping both my life's work and the view I have of human development.

One of my early clients was a flight attendant named Mary. She had come to Mel's clinic in Tarzana because of a headache she had had for several years that had resisted all other forms of treatment. At her first interview she described a tight ring of pain around her whole head, just above her ears. During our first several sessions I put her through basic relaxation exercises using biofeedback devices to help her relax various muscle groups, warm her hands, and check and lower her arousal or anxiety levels. This process seemed to help her overall mood, but did not specifically reduce her headache.

On our third session I got an idea. As she relaxed in the reclining chair in front of me, I had her pay close attention to the circular pain around her head. As she started to do this, she was immediately surprised by a subtle variety of sensations in the area that she had previously described as "just pain." I asked her to feel the ring as a whole to see if she could move the sensation up. When Mary did this, it did not move or seem to change. Undaunted, I suggested that she try to move the ring downward. As soon as she tried this, she exclaimed, "It's moving—I can feel it moving down!"

For the next fifteen minutes, she was able to slowly move the ring down through her body. She could feel the pain move with it—around her face, neck, chest, abdomen, waist, hips, all the way down to her ankles, where the progress stalled for several minutes.

"It doesn't want to move anymore," she said.

"Forget about it for a minute and just feel the breath in your lower abdomen. Relax. Don't try to force it. Just let it move," I encouraged her.

As she deepened her relaxation and focused on allowing the ring of pain to move, it slipped past her feet. All her pain was gone. She never had that headache again.

All the feelings we think are in the head are actually felt in the body. When we find and experience them, there is no need to hold them anymore.

The idea that feelings exist in the head is a very Western idea. It is related, of course, to what we know and think we know of the brain. But this is a limited view, and although the brain is of primary importance to everything we do, it is only a small part of our emotional and perceptive reality. Here in the West, when we gesture to show that we are confused, we often hold our head. In the East, people often hold their hearts when they are speaking about being confused. This body-centered approach is closer to the truth of where the feelings we call emotions come from.

All the feelings we think are in the head are actually felt in the body. When we find and experience them, there is no need to hold them anymore.

Deep Happy Inner Practice

Exploring Body Sensations

Using the approach of Deep Happy, we can learn to pay attention to what our body feels like. We can experience living in and listening to it as we go about our day.

Find a comfortable place to sit or lie down.

Start by beginning to notice how your body feels.

First notice if you are stressed, tense, or tired. You might notice that your tummy is tight or that you feel angry, frustrated, or sad. You might not even have a word for what you are feeling. That's okay. Just notice how it feels.

Notice any thoughts you might be having. Are they about whatever situation the emotions were about? Something else?

Let the thoughts be however they are.

Move your attention to your breath. Is it fast? Slow? Tense?

Gradually let your breath become deeper and deeper. Let it expand and relax in your lower abdomen. As you deepen your breathing, notice how your whole body is beginning to relax.

In the traditional Chinese medical system and in the medical systems of other countries that hold to ancient traditions of science and healing, there are associations between the internal organs and specific emotions. There are also associated areas in the body that relate to these organs. For instance, in Western scientific terms the liver can be thought of as a manager. Its job is to monitor the chemical and biological terrain and create shifts in blood chemistry, sugar levels, toxic substances, and hormones, to name a few. In traditional Asian medicine, these functions are understood, but we understand the liver to have other characteristics as well. It manages the expression of affect: the expression or retention of feelings and to some extent creativity.

When there is a sense of containment in our bodies, the liver physically, energetically, and functionally becomes tighter and denser. This can translate to tension in the upper abdomen and the diaphragm, but it can also reflect up to the shoulders and back of the neck and be experienced as emotional tension, local pain, and headaches.

As we continue to touch our tight and painful places with the light of our awareness, they gradually change and dissolve, exposing the inner part of us that is always okay.

The experience of pain can have a very clear intelligence. Not many of us want to give ourselves pain, but sometimes living with outer physical pain seems safer and easier than dealing with emotional loss or the deep angst of the concealed fear that things are going to collapse. We often unknowingly inherit these deepest concerns of living from our families as primal assumptions about life. They also show up as areas of our bodies that just don't feel good a lot of the time. They act like toxins that slowly poison us physically and lessen the quality of our lives. These dark

As we continue to touch our tight and painful places with the light of our awareness, they gradually change and dissolve, exposing the inner part of us that is always okay.

influences show themselves in patterns of pain, unconscious reaction, physical tightness, doubt, and depression. They exert themselves, altering the functioning of our organs and other body systems in negative and even destructive ways. In my clinical experience, these are the real causes of cancer, emphysema, schizophrenia, and many other end-stage diseases. These deeply physical patterns are also at the root of many political and economic conflicts. They make it so much more difficult to understand the differences between us, because rational thought and discussion rarely change these patterns from the outside in. Instead, we must become accustomed to speaking with the honest feelings from our heart. It is the guileless truth of what we feel as fellow beings that holds the possibility for real communication with each other.

So many of us live in ways that we don't comprehend about ourselves. Just yesterday morning I was doing a phone session with a woman from North Carolina named Brenda. She had had irritable bowel syndrome (IBS) for a long time and was plagued by sensitive GI symptoms. I hadn't heard from her in several months, and was surprised to receive an emergency call from her. She had been having bowel and abdominal pain on and off for a couple weeks, and it was getting worse. She had seen an internist who could offer nothing useful. During the phone session I listened very carefully to her tone of voice while questioning her about various aspects of her life. When I mentioned her husband, her voice tightened. She said that her stomach had just started to hurt again. Each time I mentioned her husband, she said things like, "He's a good guy, he's just busy all the time," or

"Whenever I'm sick or need him, he is always out." When I pointed out my observations to her, she was surprised.

It was very hard for Brenda to admit and stay with her feelings of anger and hurt. She was at the bottom of the priority list for her husband. When she would mention this to him, he would immediately respond and become temporarily supportive, but soon he would go back to discounting much of what she said and asked for. When Brenda was finally able to stay with the hurtful sensations in her abdomen, she realized that her feelings of hurt came containing her anger and frustrations; she was afraid of her husband's response. In the midst of this process, the pain in her stomach worsened until she started to sob. After a few minutes, the pain subsided and she felt clearer. This allowed her see the pattern that she lived in with her husband.

In the last part of my conversation with Brenda, it came out that her experience living at home with her mother had been almost identical. Her mother always had some kind of stomach or intestinal illness and was never able or willing to give Brenda the attention she needed. The picture became very clear: Brenda's mother was also deeply anxious and fearful, and she held most of these emotions in her pelvis and abdominal area. Brenda began to take on these dynamics in the womb. Growing up she had unknowingly learned to match her mother's feelings of constant hurt, anger, fear and submission. Unaware of this pattern, she had chosen a husband who outwardly seemed familiar, to a lesser degree exhibiting many of the habits and tendencies that her father had toward her mother. We don't choose relationships to punish or damage ourselves—I believe we choose them in an attempt to heal our old and unfinished places by continually putting ourselves in these familiar and dysfunctional situations so that eventually we can see them clearly enough to work our way out of them once and for all. The message here is that our unconscious emotional patterns are often the foundation of pain and illness. When we figure out what's going on we can get better, even in severe physical and mental conditions. In the end Brenda's husband was able to get insight into his unconscious behavior. Their relationship has drastically improved. Brenda's insight was the key.

There is something about being curious that feels very safe and seems to cut through lingering resistance. As the process of somatic self-awareness deepens, the old, creaky, deep "goo" of hurt and habit can be dissolved and eliminated by simply holding a space of awareness and acceptance around the physical location of any uncomfortable sensation. If we hold and experience whatever sensations we feel with openness, they will, in time, dissolve away. The trick is not to force them to change, but to hold the areas of sensation in a neutral awareness. From there, a healthy and interactive balance will develop, although it is common for this process to continue. In time these uncomfortable places become sources of wisdom and experience that guide and remind us of the road and the journey on which we really want to be.

My involvement with Oriental medicine and acupuncture over the last forty years has provided a very interesting window through which I understand bodies and the people who inhabit them. Surprisingly, we learned the acupuncture system from observing the body. It is a system that functions automatically in all of us. Most of the tiny bumps and bangs we get are the body trying to stimulate itself. I will illustrate this with what I remember to be my first acupuncture case a little over forty years ago in Santa Barbara.

A basically healthy woman named Carolyn came to me for what I remember to be a simple problem. During the course of her initial interview, I asked her how her periods were doing. She said that they had been very irregular until six months before, when they changed and had been perfect ever since. Our interview continued a little while longer while I tried to figure out what to do with her. It was then that I noticed a large bandage around the big toe of her left foot.

"What's going on with that?" I asked.

"You know, it's funny. A few months ago I accidentally banged it so hard that it bled. Since then, every month I do it again. I try not to, but it still happens." She answered, seeming a little perplexed with herself.

"Can you remember about when it started?" I asked.

She scrunched her face for a moment, then smiled wide with recognition.

"It was six months ago, just before Christmas," she exclaimed.

"Can you remember if it was just before or just after you had your period?" I asked.

"Now that I think about it, it was just before I had my period. I remember because my toe was so painful, I couldn't wear the new shoes I had bought for a Christmas party. I had been worried because my period was due right around then. The first day was always so painful. I had worried about it happening the day of the party, but it was completely painless—it really surprised me." Then her eyebrows twitched just a little as she got what I was getting at.

"You really think banging my toe so hard that it bleeds every month is what made my periods better?"

"Yes, I do," I told her. I explained that there are several acupuncture points on the end of the big toe that work well for bringing on a woman's period. They increase pelvic circulation and have a regulating effect on the uterus and hormones, creating relaxation and relieving emotional tension.

The big lesson here is that our body is our friend. We may not always want to hear what it has to say, but if we do we will eventually learn to trust it implicitly.

I gave Carolyn several treatments and suggested that she use a hot water bottle on her tummy the week before her period and ingest less caffeine and sweets. I suggested that she massage her toe once in a while. After that, she stopped banging her toe and her cycle was regular and pain-free.

The big lesson here is that our body is our friend. We may not always want to hear what it has to say, but if we do we will eventually learn to trust it implicitly.

Most of us have experienced little sensations—slight twinges of pain or fleeting aches—when walking or moving or just sitting around the house. Sometimes we get a little micro-itch that we absent-mindedly scratch. This is the body balancing itself, and it's a good thing. It's our body's reflexive system at work. Acupuncture is based in part on these reflexes. Without realizing it, we respond to this inner reflexive system all the time. Maybe we get an unusual urge for a hot bath or a craving for a food we have not had for a while. This is our friend, the body, telling us what it needs. The only thing required of us is that we listen and then watch the results.

You may have seen the reflex charts of the feet and the acupuncture charts that show lines and points on the body. Each of these little areas connect to different internal organs, areas, and systems. This is a fundamental adaptation system. Because of their connections, we can use them to stimulate and shift the internal functions of the body. Most of the scientific research in this area that has reached this country from Asia and Europe has been ignored.

The little areas on acupuncture charts are points. By stimulating them with our finger pressure; massaging them; using laser beams, acupuncture needles, heat, cold, ultrasound, electricity, magnets, metals, gems, and especially our inner awareness, we can send messages to the body that help it to rebalance how we feel and open embedded patterns and trauma.

I've spent thousands of hours studying and inwardly experiencing the major and minor systems in my body. If, over a period of time, I'm intensely occupied in sensing the patterns of some imbalance that I have or going into some old place inside of me in a new way, it's not uncommon for me to wake up in the middle of the night to find that I am using my breath and awareness in my sleep to connect or move something—to let it go or filter information into my upper awareness where I can understand and make use of it.

It is important to remember that although significant changes sometimes happen quickly, deeper patterns may take years or even decades to completely transform. I certainly have a few places that are long-term projects. In this regard we must accept what is and how we are, forgiving ourselves for whatever seems to be holding on. These are deeper learning opportunities and in time will show themselves to be blessings.

A few years ago, ago I was doing a month-long retreat in Shao Lin, China. The practices that we were doing were from a several-thousand-year-old Taoist lineage and were designed to open our higher energetic centers to receive higher sources of guidance and direct information. In the temple area, there were several buildings dedicated to the founders of our lineage. The statues of the lineage ancestors looked very old and wise. From their heads rose flows of energy that swirled up to clouds on which stood immortals sending down teachings and guidance. This was the main thrust of their practices—to open the higher facilities to make contact with higher dimensions. It hadn't even occurred to me that this might happen to me. But it did.

By the end of the second week I developed intense, sharp pains on the top of my head. It felt like somebody had taken a nail gun and emptied it in a circle around the upper periphery of my skull. It was excruciating, but given the circumstance I knew that it was something good and important. I paid close attention to my blood pressure, nervous system, pupil dilation, and how the rest of me felt. Eventually these sensations dissolved and brought a new openness to my higher perceptions.

If any of you reading this ever experience anything painful, startling, scary or intense during meditation, you are probably fine, but please seek attention and guidance from someone experienced in these matters.

Suffering Is Optional

We usually equate suffering with pain. Who doesn't? After all, who wouldn't suffer if they had severe back pain or knees so painful that they had difficulty walking? It is a life-changing experience when we begin to actually examine pain. This realization came during my first ten-day Vipassana retreat up in Mendocino, California in 1981. The teacher, Goenka, was accompanied by his powerful wife, Ilaichi Devi. Vipassana retreats are very strict. No talking or eye contact with anyone and twelve to fourteen hours a day of mostly sitting meditation. It was one of the most transformative meditation experiences I ever had. Sitting there with only yourself for company, very soon all of your pains, neuroses, mental editing, and evasion patterns are laid bare.

As I noticed sensations in my body, they often emerged, temporarily intensifying, waking connections to other areas, showing the deep patterns of how we deny our experience of sensing the world and our body's reaction to it. Often, after slowly dropping in to the sensations for several hours, a memory, visual image, or buried emotion would arise. Crying, laughing, and other sounds were common in the tent, where over 150 of us sank deeply into the parts of us we had thought we had left behind.

Every other day we would sit in front of Goenka and his wife. They were a powerful pair. It was never presented this way, but it seemed to me that she would energetically tune into you, seeing just whatever process you were on the edge of, then somehow she transmitted it to him and he zapped you, somehow shifting your state with his awareness. If I was feeling light and happy when I went up there, within an hour or two I would be facing the deepest, darkest clouds of emotions and energies coming out of me. If, going up there, I was on the verge of the dark abyss, soon I would feel it fall away, as meaningless as the old dried stems lying cold by the new growth of spring flowers and sparkling green shoots.

By the afternoon of the eighth day I was in excruciating pain. Every joint in my body was on fire. Sitting cross-legged for so long had never been my strong suit, and I was overwhelmed and ashamed of my lack of ability to sit with any kind of tranquility. I couldn't stand it anymore, and I just gave up and let go. In one transcendent nothing-will-ever-be-the-same moment, all the pain in my body completely disappeared. My body relaxed into the sitting posture with the ease of tired feet finding their old slippers. I felt like I could sit there for eternity and that my body was clear and formless.

A common question is, if something hurts, won't we suffer? Not necessarily. In the late 1980s, while living in the Himalayas, I was in a motorcycle accident that shredded some of the ligaments in my right knee. I have occasional flare-ups from this injury that make it difficult for me to walk without a certain amount of dull, achy, and sometimes sharp sensations. I have come to accept that my knee will not support me and carry me around like it used to, and that the sensations are just sensations. Often I can use my awareness to change or dissolve the uncomfortable feelings.

There are times when I can't. When it hurts, even sometimes keeping me up at night, it doesn't change my mood or how I feel throughout the day. I think this is mostly a matter of expectation. It all comes back to acceptance. If we can accept how things are in the moment, we can find ways to heal what needs to be healed, accept what we can't heal, and find solutions for whatever needs to be set right.

Deep Happy Inner Practice

Looking at Our Suffering and Letting It Go

If there is something that has caused you suffering, let yourself feel it now.

Feel it anywhere in your physical body, emotions, thoughts, and memories. Don't push anything away. If it has been with you, then it is already something that feels like it is inside of you.

There is nothing to fear, only to notice . . .

Look inside. Where do you feel it?

Is it from a loss? A misunderstanding? Something someone did to you or you did to them?

Do you feel physical pain?

Does it feel like a part of you is missing—a person, money, part of your body?

Let whatever it is freely go. See if you can open yourself to the acceptance of it. With your awareness, open the space where whatever is missing came from and let it become a fertile ground for something new and good. Find a way for it to be a blessing. This may be hard, but it won't be as hard as not doing it. If it is too difficult for you to let go of now, at least try to relax yourself around the issue enough so that you are not holding it all in your body. In time you will be able to let it go.

8

Emotions, Feelings, and the Felt Sense

In the depth of winter I finally learned that there was in me an invincible summer.

—Albert Camus

IN THE LANGUAGE OF our culture, the words *emotions* and *feelings* are virtually interchangeable, but for our purposes, I am going to divide them into two unique non-verbal languages. In this chapter I will also discuss the *felt sense*, which is the body's expression of intuition. This is a wonderful ability that we all have which takes all that we know consciously and unconsciously on all levels and integrates it all into a unified source for us to dip into and use however and whenever we wish. Its possibilities are as wide as we can imagine and even beyond, because even while some parts of us live under the illusion of limitation, the greater part of us is infinite. We just have to get used to letting ourselves be that big!

As we become adept at sensing and feeling the symphonies of information and communication that are ours for the listening, it becomes very useful, especially in the beginning, to have a clearer vocabulary to guide us. There is a great simplicity to this process. As it becomes second nature, the inner process of clearing, reminding, planning, understanding, and creatively developing that goes on all the time becomes like a pop-up on our inner computer screen—there whenever we need it and unobtrusive when we don't. It's like having our own personal secretary and counselor there to keep us up to date with advice on what's going on and how we are doing.

Let's start with emotions, which can be described with specific words like love, fear, anger, sadness, joy, and hate. They have specific meanings that we are familiar with, but how similar is the individual understanding that we each have for them? The word "love," for instance, is used in a very broad range of realities. "I love pizza" carries a very different tone than "the love that I feel in my heart for my child." When we say or think, "I'm afraid I might get a spot on my new white pants," it doesn't quite carry the same weight as, "I would be afraid to jump out of the plane." Yet as different as these uses might be, there are also similarities that are based on the physiology in the body from which each of these emotions stem and to which each is anchored.

Western emotional research is focused primarily on the idea that the brain is the source of emotional reality, but that belief is beginning to change. Well-known researchers like Daniel Segal realize that the physical component of emotions extends way beyond the head and into the body itself.

In the traditional Asian systems of medicine, both positive and negative emotions are linked to individual internal organs. This simple beginning forms the basis for a complex set of interlinked patterns. It's a much bigger system than we have time to go into detail about here, but I have included this chart for Chinese medicine to give you an idea that there are other systems in the world with interesting and clinically useful theories. They have millennia of experience and extensive research. When we place them in tandem with our Western approach, we are presented with a flourishing and positive view of humanity and great tools with which to relieve suffering.

Internal Organ/Emotion Relationships from Chinese Medicine

ORGANS	POSITIVE EMOTIONS	NEGATIVE EMOTIONS
Heart	Contentment/ Tranquility	Disconnected/ Nervous
Spleen	Trust/Openness/ Sincerity	Obsessiveness/ Self-Doubt
Lungs	Dignity/Courage/ Integrity	Anxiety/Grief
Kidneys	Inner Strength/ Grounded	Fear/Doubt
Liver	Kindness/Human Heartedness	Anger/Jealousy

You may have noticed that there are other organs not accounted for like the stomach, uterus, brain, intestines, and so forth. These are also included in the Asian systems, but the five organs listed above are a good start.

Deep Happy Inner Practice

Making Friends with Your Organs

Use the chart above. Pick an organ, like the lungs or liver. After relaxing and preparing yourself, begin to breathe into it, being aware of what emotional sense you are feeling there.

Experiment with each organ. First see if you can feel any of the negative attributes there—or even any of the positive ones.

Let's use the liver for an example. Tune in to it. How does it feel? Tense, tight, loose, happy, angry? Now let yourself imagine the tactile sensation of kindness. What is the physical sensation of it? When this seems clear, let yourself breathe the sensation of kindness into the area of the liver. Do this long enough to really get the feeling of it. Then you can add the second part, which is breathing out the negative energies.

Breathe the soft renewing feeling of kindness right into your liver (which is just under your ribs, in front, on the right side) and exhale out any feelings of anger or tightness. Sometimes it's hard to feel anything coming out, but give it a few minutes or a few tries. In just a short while this will become second nature. Try this with each organ. When you get more familiar with this practice, you will automatically know which organ you need to do depending on how you are feeling.

The important thing to discover is that emotions have physical locations that are grounded in the body. Even if you're skeptical about non-Western medical systems and have never considered that emotions might exist inside the body, ask yourself: how does my body feel when I'm happy or afraid or stressed? If you are in touch with your body's responses to the events of a given day, it's pretty clear that something interactive is going on in there, which matches and expands on your outer experience. Just a short time focusing on the physical sensations in your body and their link to your emotions will prove this to you more than anything I could describe in words. As you become more accustomed to feeling the increasingly subtle sensations in your body, you might be surprised at the endless layers of sensations that begin to peel off of you. You will discover that it is possible to feel any emotion anywhere in the body.

We don't need to blame ourselves for our illnesses. On a conscious level, very few of us would choose to go through a serious accident or debilitating disease. It is our responsibility to find our way out if we can. Who else's could it be? A surprising number of people get stuck on this point when they hear that illnesses might have a deeper purpose or intelligence.

There are many other descriptive words besides the ones ascribed to the organs. I Googled the phrase "descriptive words for the emotions," thinking that I might find a couple that I hadn't thought of yet, only to find what must be the world's masterpiece of emotional vocabulary. Tim Drummond of North Seattle Community College has compiled a "Vocabulary of the Emotions" which includes, by my count, 434 words in ten categories and three levels of intensity. There are forty-nine words for depression alone. They range from alienated, barren, bleak, and hopeless to subdued, uncomfortable, and unhappy.

Obviously, there are not 434 organs in the body, but those words can be applied to a combination of several organ functions. "Sympathetic" could to be a combination of heart and lungs; "appalled" could be a combination of kidneys, heart, and spleen. There are other systems that have to do with our emotional persona: polarity shifts, pre-birth and birth traumas, and inherited tendencies. On a secondary level, there are hormonal and brain/nervous system patterns, issues from toxicity, energetic polarity shifts, reflexive involvement from our teeth, and even geopathic and galactic influences that affect our mood and behavior.

The idea here is not to be overly theoretical, but to understand that emotions have very clear and specific physical realities that are linked to systemic functions and body locations. The best example of this is very well known. When someone has a heart attack, they usually have pain in their neck, shoulder, and down the inner part of their left arm. This is a very interesting medical phenomenon because in most cases, the line of referred pain down the left arm is exactly the pathway of the heart meridian of acupuncture and Chinese medicine. Heart disease is the most common serious illness in the Western world. From the view of psycho-physiology, the cause-and-effect relationship between body and mind, the main cause of heart disease is shutting down emotional sensations generated in the area of the physical heart.

From this view, when we shut off the emotions and sensations of our own heart, we also shut down our emotional connection to those around us. This negatively affects the physical heart, which in turn affects the function of the external areas of the neck, shoulders, and arm. There are specific psychological symptoms involved here as well, often including acute anxiety, apprehension, and cold sweats. In Western medicine this is thought to be from an imbalance in the sympathetic/parasympathetic system. In Chinese medicine we would also consider the imbalance through a lens that included impeded functions from the other organs and systems that affect the heart, as well as emotional causes. Contrary to what many of my high school and college teachers tried to tell me, it is clear that not all emotional experience can be expressed with words. The emotions that we feel link our body and the exact experience of the moment to our awareness and the full scope of whatever is happening.

When we use words to describe feelings and sensory presentations like art or music, they only work because they create physical associations that reverberate inside us. No matter how specifically we describe the experience of listening to a cowboy music band, the description will be far away from our sensory feast of watching the sweaty musicians in a smoke-filled, crowded bar while we tap our feet to the throbbing rhythms.

Let's clarify again what we are talking about. Emotions are mostly physical experiences that express specific states of being, like anger, love, fear, and so forth. What about the word *feelings*?

A familiar radio show host, Dr. Laura, often chides listeners who have called in for sharing what they feel and instead requests that they speak rationally and tell her what they think. Her attitude is a common prejudice that furthers behavioral pathology, disconnecting us from our emotional guidance. The promotion of that philosophy does great damage in the misguided guise of truth, and is usually put forth by those who are unable to confront and deal with their own emotional issues.

As we deepen our own innate ability to listen and respond to the unique and personal guidance inside of us, we can finally relax as we experience being lovingly held by our sacred living universe.

Choosing to listen to our head over our emotions can have long-term disorienting effects. We are built to communicate with and know ourselves by sensing how we feel. For some of us, our emotional state is conveyed to us through thoughts, but if this is done at the exclusion of "gut feeling," then we experience a form of disconnection, as the emotions offer perspective, balance, and intuition. This separation is a cause of emotional problems, because without recognizing how our body feels we have no way to fully process what might be twisting inside us.

When we are turned away from this normal process by the prejudices and propaganda of those who are fearful of their own conflicting feelings, our insecurities are stretched, making connection even more difficult. This kind of misdirection creates direct separation from the very wisdom that is designed to guide us and help us when we are in trouble or doubt.

As we deepen our own innate ability to listen and respond to the unique and personal guidance inside of us, we can finally relax as we experience being lovingly held by our sacred living universe.

Each of us has a unique style of perception and action. Some systems divide this down into thinking, feeling, and action. We do all three, but as individuals we can do them in a different order. Some think first, some feel first, and some act first. Some of us are more visual, more auditory, or more tactile, but we all integrate these three sensory abilities. In spite of these variations, I have found no difference in anybody's ability to perceive subtle sensations in their body. I expected this to be a problem and I'm still on the watch for it, but I haven't worked with anyone who did not get better and more adept at listening to and feeling themselves—and I've worked with thousands of people.

In addition to the specific character of each feeling, there is a pervasive and deeply primal somatic language of sensation and tone. This is the language of animals and instinct—the ability to function by sensing rather than using intellect. This process can work in *all* situations. Sometimes when we enter a room or meet someone new, we get a specific feeling that lets us know the quality of what is going on. This may be an obviously good or bad feeling, or it may express something that takes more sensing to figure. Imagine living your life with continual access to this level of direct awareness. It is already working—you just have to notice it.

We all use this non-verbal sense every time we go to a restaurant. Sitting at the table or counter, we pick up the menu and scan the various possibilities for our meal. If we pay attention, we notice that there is a very clear feeling in our abdomen pertaining to what our body would like to eat and how it feels about each item we think about. We look down the list: Cobb salad, macaroni and cheese in a butter sauce, sautéed vegetables and brown rice, rib-eye steak, salad, tofu. Each of us will get a particular sensation in our stomach for each food. You probably did just reading this list.

The inner sense of "deep knowing" is never one of salesmanship or coercion. It never pushes except in dire matters of survival. Even then it is just a sharp call to action. It's the excited quality of the inner unrelenting salesmanship of the voice in our head and the intensity of the prompting that should alert us to pay closer attention to whatever it is that we are thinking about doing. This "wave of questionable intent" is usually accompanied by thoughtful and seemingly rational inner comments and justifications like "You deserve this," "It will make you feel better," or the famous, "I have been looking for this (you) all my life." It is possible that these ideas might occasionally be true, but their inner presentation has a very different feel to it. It's the sense of disconnected excitement that creates the "snappy sizzle" and "burning desire" and urges us forward beyond a normal sense of balance and way beyond who we really are that signals caution. The "sizzle" and "burn" can be fun when we are young or on vacation or when we might just need to blow off steam. But in the long term they create obstacles when we are trying to create a good and steady life or find financial solvency.

Something is wrong and I don't know what it is.

—John Mayer

Sometimes it is more difficult for us to know and sense the truth of our situation. Usually this occurs when we reach a point where things are just not working and we don't know why. It is then that we must really work to pay attention. If we find that we are not happy, there is a good reason hiding somewhere under the edge of our perception, waiting to be noticed. There are always little clues trying to get our attention. These could be the tiniest moments of anger or frustration, maybe a slight pain or ache somewhere that just popped up when our lover or boss said something.

I recently had a conversation with a friend who had just initiated a separation from her husband after being together for fourteen years of marriage. He had started to date other people and she was having second thoughts about what she wanted. She really felt confused.

I suggested that she let all the voices inside her speak—that she let anything and everything come out of her, no matter how small and petty, selfish, mean, and even nasty. I told her to listen to all the positive parts: married a long time, father of their children, good lover, and so forth. As she did this, she realized that the things that she thought she was angry at him for were really a contrived excuse for her to be able to live alone for awhile—that she was tired and needed space to find her way again. This was not the answer that she had expected, but as soon as this realization hit her she was able to feel at ease again and creatively figure out a way to accommodate both her needs and those of her husband.

Our body and consciousness want to unite—it's a biological imperative.

Our body and consciousness want to unite—it's a biological imperative.

It is fundamental to accept that we get to be ourselves, just as we are.

Reaching a higher understanding actually has a direct physical reference. There is a part of our brain, at the top of the head, called the anterior cingulate gyrus. One of its important functions is to define viewpoints big enough to hold and unite seemingly opposing concepts and realities. We automatically use this pre-wired part of us any time we seek answers and solutions that consider wider vistas of possibility.

The Buddhists teach that at the core of everyone is their Buddha nature—the innate essence of wisdom and radiant compassion that is the true foundation of life and consciousness. This is nothing we have to buy or even develop—we just have to peel back the layers of unconsciousness and habit, and there it is. When get better at remembering that each of us has the essence inside, we get better at living and connecting with each other from that sacred place. This is Deep Happy

As our daily experience of the interconnectedness of life broadens, we find that we have a wonderful ability and responsibility to share, without ceremony or pretense, feeling good.

Whether it's the tyranny of our own past traumas that deny us the freedom to live from our heart, or the tyranny of the social and political structures of our time that deny us, it is our innate ability, right, and duty to shake off the illusions of our restraints. This not only serves our own life and purpose, but it reminds and encourages everyone around us and prepares the world for the global shift in frequency that is already upon us.

We always have the ability to change our inner state. No matter how difficult or challenging our situation is, every one of us has the pre-wired ability to reach in and grab the balm of the deep essence within us. With a little practice, we can get clear, calm, and connected, no matter how we are battered, shattered, and obstructed.

I want to mention here a little bit on positive energy. An article in the *New York Times* last year reported that "Happiness Is Contagious!" If you are in a good mood and share it as you go about your day, the effect will be passed from person to person for as long as four hours. Imagine the unexpected effects that this simple process could have.

The power in this phenomenon derives from the authenticity and depth of the feeling state that we are sharing. The truer and more pervasive it is, the more the feeling can spread. What would be the cumulative effect of the deliberate spread of contagious happiness after, say, a hundred years?

As our daily experience of the interconnectedness of life broadens, we find that we have a wonderful ability and responsibility to share, without ceremony or pretense, feeling good.

9

Intuition

There is no logical way to the discovery of these elemental laws. There is only the way of intuition, which is helped by a feeling for the order lying behind the appearance.

—Albert Einstein

Cease trying to work everything out with your minds. It will get you nowhere. Live by intuition and inspiration and let your whole life be revelation.

—Eileen Caddy

EVERYBODY HAS INTUITION. It is how our inner self speaks to us when our frontal cortex isn't looking. I have written so much about developing our inner skills of sensitivity and listening, but intuition seems to happen to everybody, even when we have "tuned out, closed down, and gone to bed." Intuition can speak to us in our dreams. It can get through to us even when we have had too much of a good old-vine zinfandel. It can and will move our body and mouth before we have a chance to realize it. If our intuition wants to tell us something, it will find a way. The more important the message, the louder and longer it will persevere until the message is received.

Everyone has had experiences with intuition. Perhaps you knew who was calling when you heard the phone ring or had a feeling that a friend was coming over just before they knocked on your door. If you ask around enough, you will inevitably hear accounts of very normal folks doing "amazing" things like knowing their child was in an accident or not getting on a plane that later crashed. Intuition is where Deep Happy lives, because it is where we experience first-hand the width and breadth of our oneness and connection with life and the universe.

It is very common for me to get an urge to drop what I am doing and turn on the TV only to find that a program has just started on a topic I have been researching or am interested in. Several weeks ago, while working on this book, I kept getting a feeling that I wanted to have lunch at a local restaurant. We had food in the house, but I kept thinking of a Cobb salad. It didn't occur to me that this was anything more than a desire for lunch. By 12:30 the subtle pull was too strong, and I had to go down the hill to the Corte Madera Café. I walked in, sat down, and ordered. A few minutes later, a man walked by my table, nodded, and walked out the door. It took me a moment to recognize who he was: the service manager at the local Honda dealer. I had been there the week before, helping an elderly Buddhist nun friend to resolve a serious problem with her car. The manager had given us a very difficult time and in fact had stormed away, calling me an ass. Just as I remembered who he was, he came back in the restaurant and headed right for my table. I wasn't sure what to expect, but as he reached me he slowed down and extended his hand.

"I'm sorry," he said."It was a really bad day and I just lost it. Please accept my apology."

He then handed me a card good for a free lube.

Of course I accepted his apology, and he told me that he felt so relieved and thanked me. An interesting addendum to this was that in the aftermath of him calling me an ass, the dealership became extra helpful in resolving my friend's problem. If we are aware of the big picture and keep a balance while letting reality take its often surprising course, unexpected things happen, especially if we don't get in the way. During the heated discussion with the manager, my intuition kept telling me to just let things percolate. When he finally yelled and went away, I instinctively knew that the obstacles to the resolution of our situation had just dissolved—and they had.

The incident in the café was not particularly profound, but it allowed the release of tension between two people. My intuition let me know in a gentle way that something useful could happen if I listened and followed up on what I heard. Because my mind was so busy working on this book about being happy and sensitive, I missed being directly sensitive to the guidance that was offering specific information. So it chose to get my attention the old-fashioned-way, with food! With me that strategy works every time!

Intuition is not some magical power, although it may seem like it sometimes. It is actually the culmination of all our intelligence, body awareness, wisdom, and perceptive ability working together. In the most basic sense, intuition is our body sensing something and then telling our head about it.

In the early 1970s, when I was still living in Santa Barbara, I had friends who lived on boats in the beautiful harbor there. One day I was visiting John, who lived on an old Chinese flat-bottomed junk, and I met someone whose story has never left me. I am sorry that I don't remember his name or exactly what he looked like, though I remember him needing a shave, with tanned leathery skin and eyes that were at the same time piercing, very aware, and yet soothing. This man had spent the previous six years sailing the world in a forty-two-foot sloop. For four of those years he had been completely alone.

We talked for several hours and then I never saw him again. Much of the conversation involved what it had been like to be alone in the vastness of the sea for so long. The story that I remember is this:

There had been a minor problem with the engine of the man's boat, which he had not been able to fix because one of his wrenches had slipped overboard during an intense storm. One morning, while sailing in the south Pacific, he woke up "knowing" that there was another ship eighty miles northwest, heading due east, and that it had the wrench he needed. He knew clearly that it was in the second drawer of a chest under the gangway.

He said that it had taken him a day and a half to catch up with that ship, and yes, the wrench had been right where he had "seen" it. He also mentioned that the crew on the boat didn't seem the least bit surprised when he asked if he could use wrench in the second drawer.

At that time, in my early twenties, I had little understanding of how these things worked, but I was very intrigued by them. I asked him how he thought that he was able to know the wrench was there and to so finely tune in to the exact course and location of the other boat. He said that out there in the immensity of the ocean there was no interference. That without all the things to get in the way, what *was* there stood out. Especially above the water, there were no people, animals, power lines, or television broadcasts to clutter the wide emptiness—only the sky.

Later the man talked about sensing a presence around or under the boat, sometimes staying nearby for hours. This would often culminate, he said, in a huge whale emerging from the water. The whales would stay right next to the boat, sometimes letting him touch them with his feet or hands if he leaned way over the side. Once, he and his boat were pounded by a storm that forced him to do little else for three days but stay below deck and hang on. At night he had to lash himself to his bunk, exhausted, hungry, and dehydrated. After the storm was over, he was reclining in the sun on deck when two huge whales appeared on each side of his boat and stayed for several hours, singing. He said that the sounds and energy were both comforting and healing. He fell asleep listening to them and woke up feeling completely refreshed. The experience with the whales left him with a feeling of deep and sacred thankfulness at the interconnectedness of life.

Whether to the songs of whales or to some seemingly mundane event, our connection to the immensity of all that is always speaking to us. Mental rigidity and doubt make it more difficult to access. Obviously we can talk ourselves into certain things, especially if we are very attached to the idea of them, but if we allow our intuition to express itself and then let ourselves experiment with it, we will soon be able to trust it in the same way we trust our ability to distinguish hot objects from cold ones.

Intuition also speaks to us directly through our body. It is the culmination of our entire felt sense, taking all the available information from all possible sources being channeled and organized into a simple and coherent message. As I have said before, it can come through thoughts, words, sentences, feelings, internal pictures, or impressions that outer images and events remind us of, and it can directly cause seemingly unconscious actions in our body.

One sunny morning many years ago I was driving down a street in southern California in a borrowed VW bus, listening to reggae music on the radio. All of a sudden, without any warning, I watched my hands yank the wheel of the car to the left and make a turn onto a side street. I was dumbfounded. I literally asked myself out loud, "What the #@* are you doing?" Shaking my head at what I thought was my own stupidity, I made a right turn at the first corner. I was just about to make the next right turn to get back to my original route when I saw someone standing on the corner whom I recognized from my past. It was Lisa, the sister of my best friend Mark from high school back in Michigan. I had been hoping to get back in touch with their family for some time, and had had no way of finding them. Driving down the street, something in me sensed her there. Apparently I was busy listening to the radio in reggae la-la land, so my inner self decided to get the message across before it was too late and she and I both passed that moment where we could easily meet. We have stayed in touch ever since.

I have always been interested in the experiences of hunters, though I am not one myself. Something about hunting calls to the shadows of ancestral memories inside me as a latent human domain. I am not a big meat eater, but sometimes when I eat a piece of meat or a freshly caught fish I wonder how different life would be if we still had to hunt for our food.

I have been able to talk with two aboriginal hunters, an Inuit Eskimo, and tribesmen from the plains of Africa. I have also had a number of conversations with modern hunters from North America. I wanted to get a feel for what it was like for them to hunt. These conversations gave me a deeper understanding and respect for it. The experience of these hunters was not so different, though the experience of the Canadian was less obviously spiritual.

Both the Inuit and the Kenyan talked of sensing the animals from far away. It wasn't just their movements, but also the feeling of their spirit and even personality. They both recalled in their own but similar way that the trick was to become as neutral as possible. They had to hold in their personal sense of self as if they had no unique existence of their own, letting themselves become invisible of sight, sound, smell, and feel. The more they could be transparent, the less likely that the prey they were stalking would sense them. They also mentioned the importance of holding a reverence and thankfulness for the animal that would give up its life so that they could eat. A Canadian said that he could feel the animals as points on a map if he was able to empty his mind and connect to his surroundings. It seems clear from these accounts that our innate intuition has been an important survival skill that allowed us to function in a more primitive time.

Today, intuition is just as useful for almost anything, but especially creativity. Both my mother and grandmother were artists. When I was younger I worked doing metal sculpture and design in New York. I play several instruments and have worked as a craftsman in wood and stained glass; made knives; and wrote poems, songs, and now a book. There is very little that revs me up as much as the creative process. Whenever I can play my guitar or write at my computer, letting myself be wide open and receptive, I am Deep Happy. For me this is intuition at its best—guiding, surprising, setting the tone and tempo in whatever medium it is speaking through. While I was writing *Deep Happy,* I would set my intention at night before I went to bed. I usually woke up early with ideas of what I wanted to write, not as finished chapters but as a happy soup of words, feelings, and ideas. I made my green tea, sat down at my computer, and it usually began to flow. When it didn't, I would take some time to find my center and humility and let the boundaries between the identity of my personal self dissolve and unite into my "big self." Playing one of my guitars or Indian flutes, going for a walk with our dogs, feeling the morning sun on my face or any sensory non-cortical activity helps me to find the creative groove, and lets the "me" get out of the way.

As a teacher I depend on intuition to connect me in just the right way to my audience. Without thinking too much about it, I trust my intuitive connection to help me find the words, nuance, and stories to connect me with my clients. I have learned that if I know what I am teaching, I can "just let it rip." For short talks and teaching, I usually have little planned for what I am going to talk about. As the time approaches, I can literally feel ideas, topics, and stories organizing themselves inside of me. I feel my consciousness connecting to those who will be attending, in some non-verbal way linking their needs and questions with the energy of the time and day to my abilities and experiences. In this way something real can occur as a group creation.

Our intuition can prepare the way for us and to keep watch on all that is swirling in the orbits of action and consequence.

Our intuition can prepare the way for us and to keep watch on all that is swirling in the orbits of action and consequence.

Each of us is an organic machine of incredible complexity—complexity of biology, emotions, karma, and stresses, all combined with the changing influences of the seasons, magnetic fields, solar radiation, local geopathic effects, and much more. It is probably impossible to consciously keep track of all of this, but the intuitive process can quickly make us aware of what to do with it all. When I am with a client, I hold an intent to assist them in whatever way will best serve them, while at the same time letting pictures, impressions, and phrases appear in the empty field of my awareness.

I have followed this process long enough to trust it; I usually know when I am off track. I can tell I'm off because what is showing up in my mind will be confused and jumbled. I can be thrown off if something about my client or their story is triggering me in some way. When I realize this is happening, I push back my own stuff and then recalibrate the situation.

Developing Intuition

Intuition is something we can develop consciously. It is already there, working behind the scenes, so we already have a lot to build on. This ongoing process furthers Deep Happy.

Usually a good way to start is to make a list of the times in your life when you felt or heard the voice of your own intuition. It may be that you are used to using other words: "got a hunch or a feeling, *knew* something, had to do something," and so forth. These are all the same as intuition. It's a non-logical process of directly knowing or sensing something. Sometimes it's a vague feeling and at other times it can be very detailed information.

I remember one spring nineteen years ago when I had been single for a while and was wondering how long it would be before I got into a relationship again. Within a day I got a very clear impression that by the end of the following September I would meet someone. I was a little off—the first week of the following October I met the woman who would be the mother of my son.

Just like learning to use a computer or play a musical instrument, we can become masters of our intuition. The best first step is to just start paying more attention to body sensations, especially the ones in the abdomen. "Gut feeling" is not just a saying; it is also an exact description of where we can access how our bodies feel about something.

We can actually program intuition to help us in very specific ways. The basic premise of this is having a clear intent that supersedes conflicting voices inside you. A mundane example is having your body wake you up at an exact time. When going to bed, look at the clock. Then see the time that you want to wake up. Be clear and strong in your mind that that is what you want to do, and you will wake up. After doing this for a while, your inner clock will wake you to the minute. In this same way, all the various points of focus that we have within us constantly shift what our intuitive guidance provides us. Because of this, it is important for each of us to take time to ourselves to just sit or walk and let our inner voices speak to us. If this is not something you regularly do, you may find an entire chorus trying to speak, each with a different idea. Let them all speak or yell, but especially listen to the ones that whisper. They are usually the most important ones. After "letting the dogs out," your inner symphony will relax and the real voices from your essence will make themselves known to you.

To fully awaken your intuitive abilities, you must make regular time for this process to work. It may take a week, a month, or a year, but in the meantime you will have many interesting insights. Eventually you to get to a place where listening to your intuition becomes as second nature as searching the Internet. Sometimes people are doubtful or resistant about learning something new and unique. To that I usually answer: We will all be dead soon. We must wake up and live in this particular existence while we can. Life moves quickly. Life responds to life. When we let the fire of our healthy and connected will and passion come alive, the universe will respond, and opportunities and possibilities will help us facilitate whatever it is that we must do. How else could it be?

Deep Happy Inner Practice

Programming Your Software

Pick something that you want to experiment with. Let your inner guidance tell you what it is. Follow these directions and see what happens. Pick something safe for now.

Listen to your thoughts and feelings for a while until you notice a recurring topic.

Listen more carefully to the tone and style of your guidance.

Is it a specific voice or feeling?

Do you get an inner picture or some combination of thoughts, feelings, and images?

Discover what your particular channel is and what it feels like.

Have an intent and notice when your inner computer is prompting you. Try and listen when it speaks.

Think of times you heard a message but did not follow it. The more you pay attention and trust it, the more it will be there for you.

Play and experiment with it!

For me it is like the little areas of information on the home page on my web browser, only inside my head. An area for news, one for weather, and so forth—only in my inner sensing/knowing areas there are places that tell me things I am feeling but haven't paid attention to. I often get specific information about certain people or places that I need to talk to or go to. During the day I get little snippets to add to whatever project I'm working on.

All consciousness is connected. So are you.

Guides, Teachers, Divine Beings

Guides, teachers, divine beings—whatever you want to call them—are just other channels that we turn to simply by being receptive. We make our choices by the level, focus, and tone of our consciousness, intent, hopes, and prayers. The clearer we become within ourselves, the more we can call other specific sources and communicate with them.

I woke one morning several years ago with the decision to change the context of a relationship I was in with a woman. I was living in a large house on a hill in Stinson Beach that had been mostly empty for years. I had often thought that I sensed a presence there. By midday I had made up my mind and decided to call her that evening. Almost as soon as I thought this, I heard a voice literally yell in my ear. "Don't break up with her now. You have not finished your work together."

All consciousness is connected. So are you.

The voice continued to yell loudly in my left ear.

"Not now, don't break up with her."

Though I have had many very specific messages in my life, that was the only time I had them yelled to me.

So I didn't, and in hindsight the additional time together was beneficial for both of us.

Most of my life I have had guidance and inner assistance, ideas, feelings, and hunches that came at important times. I did not even realize it until I was older and had a chance to reflect back on some of the things that happened to me. I have already written about some of them in other parts of this book. When I was with my teacher Dabsang Rinpoche in Nepal, this level of inner communication became so common that I stopped thinking of it as anything but normal. Even after his passing my connection with him has continued.

One morning more than ten years after he died, I received an early call from my friend Margo, a psychic and professor of literature who lived in San Diego. This was the year after my first divorce, and I was very shut down and unhappy.

"I got a message from your teacher, last night in meditation," she told me. "He wants you to do certain practices and be celibate for a year. He told me that he would knock on your bedroom window tonight at 2 AM." She also told me the specific practices I was to do. I should mention here that Margo was not very familiar with Tibetan Buddhism. She had never met my teacher, but had commented once after seeing his picture that she felt a strong presence when she tuned in to him. Yet she was able to relay very precise details about the particular practices that Rinpoche had instructed me in. I had never talked with her or anyone else about them. There was no way that she could have known about them in any other way. Margo is very sensitive and had always been right in whatever she had told me before. That night I was woken up at 2 AM by a knocking sound on my window, which, by the way, was on the second floor. I felt a strong presence in the room, which stayed with me for the next six months as I worked through the results and repercussions of the work and practices he had instructed me to do.

10

Relationships and Sex

Fortune and love favor the brave.

—Ovid

I know a man who gave up smoking, drinking, sex, and rich food. He was healthy right up to the day he killed himself.

—Johnny Carson

HUMANS ARE BASICALLY HERD animals. We assume our illusion of individuality, grazing under our separate tree, but in the evening when the rest of the animals begin to find their way back to the barn, often without realizing it we move with them, telling stories of our day.

Many years ago, after my divorce, I decided to research relationships and all the different theories about them to figure out what happened to my own marriage. I thought I knew about myself and something about the dynamics of how people interacted with each other, yet I watched the dream of love and family dissolve into a nightmare of arguments, conflict, and pain. In the end it was like trying to hold water in your hands—no matter what you do, it finds a way to leak out. I resolved to learn about them and to provide a better relationship model for my son. After several years, I ended up teaching relationship classes for a group involved with conscious relationships. From this experience and a great deal of further research, I developed clinical protocols based on a reengineering of the physiology I observed of human bonding, attachment, desire, and disassociation.

It is a common human desire to hold someone close, to feel them merge with your core, languishing in an ocean of human connection. It sounds healing and fulfilling, but for quite a few of us, this experience eventually becomes challenging. It takes a deep level of personal healing and awareness to sustain that level of intimacy and retain a clear and healthy sense of self. If we are not used to emotional intimacy, we may need some time and personal work to stay comfortably in the presence and connection of real intimacy.

When I reached the age of thirty I began to think that girls did not like me. They would seem interested, but then they would go away. One day I realized that as I pulled them toward me with one hand, I energetically pushed them away with the other. This was a revelation! When I tried pulling them with both hands, it was a stampede. So I tried pushing them back with both hands to a distance that I felt comfortable with. Even though I desperately wanted someone close, I realized I wasn't ready. Over the next few months I experimented and found a balance of emotional connection. Over the next several years I consciously developed a succession of learning relationships that allowed me to feel safe with increasing levels of intimacy. Even though in the beginning I wanted the intensity of intimacy, in time I found the right combination of emotional connection and space that allowed an intimate synergy in my relationships.

The fear and attraction of intimacy is a common theme in new relationships. When our feelings about meeting someone new are exciting and make us feel giddy and a little or a lot crazy, there are forces beneath the surface of our awareness working to bring us back to the old patterns of unconscious programming that are driving the attraction. Being in love is an unforgettable experience. It can be like a drug that energizes us and makes us feel alive and whole. But if you look back to the relationships that started as incredibly intense magnetic encounters of mutual emotional and physical attraction, you might notice that not many of them held together in the long run. Though they are certainly wonderful while they last, the downside is usually heartache, dismay, or worse. With a larger perspective relationships can be great opportunities to recognize what happened (the real purpose of why we attract these kinds of interactions) and begin to sort things out a little more clearly for next time.

When we meet someone who is actually a good match for us, it usually feels different. When I met my wife Conde, I felt a gentle happy glow and an inner knowing that *something* was going on. I had the sense of being energized, but I never felt disconnected from myself or lost track of who I was. Several weeks after we first got together, I attended a five-day meditation retreat in Santa Cruz. By the end of the second day, it occurred to me that where I wanted to be was back home with Conde. I didn't have to talk myself into it or rationalize my feelings (leaving a retreat is something I had never done)—I just knew that was what I needed to do. And I did. We were married almost two years to the day from that weekend.

Learning to trust what our inner senses tell us becomes very useful in any kind of relationship, no matter what the connection turns out to be. When we meet someone new, we get an instant feeling about them that is always on the money—if we pay attention to the little nuances of it. As we get to know the new person, things we learn about them may overshadow our original sense of them, but it is handy and wise to trust our initial perception and factor that in as the relationship progresses.

Knowing and trusting our feelings in romantic relationships is vital. Primal signals like smell can announce the truth of our physical attraction and the psychological, karmic, and energetic links that we have with each other. Much has been said of how our appearance and smell is changed by cosmetics and even surgery. It can be hard to know who we are really getting when we meet someone.

I read an article that talked about how fruit flies mate for life. It mentioned how fruit flies, who choose their mate by smell, became confused and couldn't find their mate after they have been given antibiotics under laboratory conditions. It was thought that the antibiotics altered the colonies of microorganisms, changing their metabolism and in turn their basic smell. I couldn't help wondering if our modern overuse of antibiotics and other pharmaceuticals has changed our basic genetically encoded smell to such a degree that we now have trouble recognizing compatible mates. Sometimes incredibly small and unsuspected influences can make huge shifts in our world.

Our lives are entwined. Whether we are friends, lovers, business associates, fellow students, enemies, competitors, co-conspirators, or even just seatmates on a plane headed for Timbuktu (I've been there, it's overrated), our lives are linked in obvious and unseen ways. Whatever our experience, our suffering or well-being is part of the collective felt experience of humanity on the planet and even beyond.

We are all family. Think what that really means. Feel it in your marrow!

We are all family. New research in physics and cosmology that disrupts our old theories of the big bang and the gravitational organization of the universe is revealing an immense galactic and universal linking through electromagnetic flows and plasma seas.

Whether you believe the assertions that every one of us on this planet came from South Africa, that creation occurred eight thousand years ago, or that we are all star children, descendants from travelers from other extraterrestrial worlds, the meaning is the same. We are all family. If we expand our observations and include existing research and what we know about the nature of reality, our family will include all life, all consciousness. The aboriginal peoples of the world count water, plants, earth, and even rocks as family.

We are all family. Think what that really means. Feel it in your marrow!

Science has described many areas where we interact constantly with each other. Some of these are well known—we share bacteria, viruses, and the other infinitesimally small creatures with our body (90 percent of the cells in our body are non-human; the non-human ones are just very small).

When my son was in elementary school, we had a daily sampling of all the wonderful bugs that were shared at school, instructing my son's immune systems and testing our own. But this is only the beginning—there are many other ways we are just learning about how biological forms interact.

Every time we touch or come near someone, there is a great probability that some of their DNA will come into contact with our own. In addition to DNA, the hormones and pheromones of friends and strangers yell symphonies of possibilities to us in a micro language of chemistry and instinct. Besides direct contact there is also contact within the morphogenic resonance or field of consciousness.

Many years ago, I had a wonderful and quirky cat named Bert. He was never a perfect specimen of health—he was always little frail, and one eyeball was a bit smaller than the other. I loved him anyway. At the time I had a small house in a tiny rural town in northern California, Cazadero. It was just across the road from a large stream and the neighborhood was filled with cats. Bert eventually came down with feline leukemia, an autoimmune disease where the kidneys stop producing a chemical that normally sends messages to the marrow inside the bones to make red cells for blood. About 10 percent of the cats in that town eventually came down with it, and my beloved Bert died after only a few months.

As we have seen, in Chinese medicine one of the energetic functions of the kidneys is to connect the ancestral momentum of the two families that we come from to us as a source of biological direction. After Bert died, I realized that a field of primal mutual awareness connected all the cats in the area. There were too many cats for the relatively small area to support. So in order to preserve the biological integrity, my thinking is that the weaker ones were culled by the collective cat consciousness in the most humane way possible. Bert felt no pain, just a slow weakening of his system as he became more and more anemic.

I am sure that to some of you this sounds way out there. But if you think about the life of our species, our *prime directive* is to survive and become better at our adaptation to living on earth. Think of each living thing as a cell and their species as the body they are a part of. What would be more critical to that end than a mutual sensing of the condition and process of each of the individuals and how they affect the whole? The microcosm mirrors the macrocosm.

What would it mean to believe this perspective, to acknowledge our individuality as part of a conscious whole? It could mean that when we choose to be a friend to someone or to love someone, let alone share our bodies, we may not just be acting as individuals. There is a strong possibility that we may be responding to a pervasive genetic or transcendent guidance of what may not just be good for us, but may also be good for our species.

How can we explore this? Very simple. We begin to notice our inner cues, all the micro sensations and feelings that either agree or disagree with what our head tells us. We let our body show us its response to all the biological, emotional, and energetic signals that come from every person and every living thing. In this unseen dimension, where a deeper and primal truth is always present, the tone and timbre of words has more meaning than the actual substance of what is said. Facial expressions and posture offer unseen counterpoints, often reversing the meaning of what is said on the surface of the conversation.

There was research done in the 1970s that showed that when someone is speaking in front of a group, the mouth of each person in the audience moves simultaneously and imperceptibly in sync with the words of the speaker. This is because the brain waves and neural signals that moved meaning and words out through the speaker's mouth also moved the mouths of each person in the room. From functional and energetic medicine (see the work of James Oshman, et al.) we know that each cell, organ, body part, and system emits a frequency and tone that the bodies of everyone within a certain range can feel.

Several years ago I read a book report by Christian De Quincy in the *Journal of the Institute of Noetic Science.* It told a story about an anthropologist in England in the mid-1800s. This gentleman had heard about an expedition going to Guinea to visit a tribe that had never seen white people before. Somehow this anthropologist managed to get there a month or so before the English expedition. He was able to travel inland to find the unique tribe.

The reason this anthropologist used all of his resources to get there first was to witness the moment-to-moment unity that each member of the tribe had with each other. If someone woke up one morning feeling out of sorts, the whole tribe would focus on them until they felt back in harmony. The unity of the group was the most important thing. A month after the anthropologist reached the tribe, the British sailors arrived and took over the area. One month after that, many members of the tribe had schizophrenic breaks. They couldn't fathom the harsh culture and emotional distance of the seamen.

I have no expectation that our world will ever reach such a point of sensitivity—I'm not even sure it would be a good thing to be that enmeshed. But I do know that feeling loved and safe and being held within a community as family, friend, and equal would be a medicine for most of the ills of our society.

Soul Mates

I would like to add a few things here about "soul mates." I believe that we can have more than one soul mate, and those relationships are not always easy! Many people I know who have met their soul mate have agreed unequivocally that oftentimes, being in that relationship was very difficult—for many it was not something they wanted to do in the long term. I know in saying this that I am cutting across the grain of hope for all of you who are seeking a soul mate, so I will explain this further. A soul mate is someone who shows up in our life to touch us so deeply and at such a critical time that we can't help but shake free of all that keeps us from being and expressing our essence into the world. A common experience when first meeting our soul mate is a lovely opening of some portal between the two of you. When I met Annie, it was not exciting—but it was obvious that something unseen and powerful connected us. Several years after our first meeting, we actually got together.

Annie and I first met at a conference on spirituality and consciousness at a well-known center in upstate New York.

She and I were both in relationships at the time. I don't think either of us initially thought about getting together romantically. We had a very comfortable and energizing connection. She had come to a couple of my workshops, and we had talked about working together sometime. She is a neuropsychologist specializing in jury assessment in San Diego—bright, lovely, aware, and ardent about the inner workings of personality. We had a great conversation on the phone a month or so after the conference, but then we both got busy with our lives. A year later we ran into each other again at the same conference. I was with my wife and Annie was with her boyfriend, who was also presenting there that year. We had surprisingly little contact, but the feeling was even stronger the few times that we did get to talk. The next year, we met again. This time the energy was stronger still. By then my marriage was over, so I commented on how strong the connection was between us and asked if she was available. She said no, that she was still in a relationship. After that, though, the fuse was lit. A week later she emailed me to say that she had broken up with her boyfriend. She had not wanted to say anything before because they were still working out the details. A few days later, after ten phone calls in a few days, I flew down to San Diego.

The sudden intensity of our meeting initially pushed me into a certain disconnection, but within a short time it seemed to relax. As the months progressed, almost every weekend one of us would travel to see the other. Over time we developed a very close working relationship, often consulting each other on clients. The unity of our bond was certainly one of the highlights of my life. Gradually, as winter approached, the real purpose of our work together began to emerge.

Annie had grown up in Maine within a very restrictive "down east" family mentality. She felt contained, edited, and held in for most of her life, and she needed space and freedom to heal. My primary issue was one of abandonment. I needed connection and intimacy to move beyond my hurts and emotional limitations. You can guess the fundamental difficulty and also healing possibility between us. As our situation transitioned, the powerful love and connection between us made it possible for us to move the relationship beyond the romantic to a deep friendship that exists to this day. We are now in happy strong relationships with other people, and we will always have a deep love for each other that is the foundation of the connections that helped us both to heal and move into balanced and sustainable relationships. She was at my wedding with Conde, and is our mutual friend.

When I taught relationship classes, I discovered something that I used to pass on to my students. In any kind of beginning relationship, it is useful to not limit the nature of the relationship with words that carry a lot of expectations. Words like "boyfriend," "girlfriend," "mate," "long-term relationship," and so on dictate a certain reality that in truth may be more fluid than we first realize. Sensing our way through, moment to moment, it is so important to be open to the truth of how the relationship might be changing and growing. From this perspective there are no bad or failed relationships. Relationships are what they are, the natural emerging creative connection between two or more people responding to whatever is true, real, and possible.

Relationships can be easy if we let them and each other be who and how we are, holding them together with acceptance, freedom, and the deepest love we can muster.

I have worked with several people involved in long-term relationships who have questioned whether or not their relationship should continue. After a while, in most relationships, the fire and even the fun can fade in the face of the pressures of work, family, and the individual growth. Satisfying physical and emotional connections can fall away after years of held-in communications and the denial of our own needs. The exact same process that Deep Happy is about can uncover and dissolve the held-in emotions and energies that are usually at the root of it all.

Sex

Sex is a huge coming together of the genetic, historic (sometimes hysteric), social, cultural, physical, and emotional perspectives, intents, and abilities of two completely different streams of life and consciousness. When I hear someone say something like, "As soon as we met, we just clicked. It was like we had known each other forever," I can't help but wonder at all the history, karma, and biology that went into that connection.

Of course as we get older and more mature, it is easier to override some of these primal concerns of sexuality, physical attraction, and even romantic love with pragmatic concerns of compatibility and the mutual ability to live a satisfying life together. This can be a successful and happy choice that allows us to integrate our needs with ones that serve the reality of our current life situation. There is no doubt that people can choose whether they want to be happy; after all, choice is one of the basic premises of Deep Happy. But I think it is important to ask the question: Do we really need to leave important parts of us out of the equation just to be happy? I would say that the answer is a resounding not necessarily! But as we gain a wider perspective, some of our needs will undoubtedly fall away, allowing others that more easily fit who we have become to take their place.

Relationships can be easy if we let them and each other be who and how we are, holding them together with acceptance, freedom, and the deepest love we can muster.

Most of us know couples that may not have been sexually or physically intimate with each other for a long time. Perhaps intimacy was never part of their relationship at all. Many of these couples seem perfectly happy, but of course many don't. In relationships, differing sexual needs and styles can be a huge problem if they are not openly and lovingly resolved with communication, non-judgment, patience, and creativity. When this kind of healing fails to happen, couples can either close off or even become openly antagonistic toward each other. There are so many shadows and cultural pressures involving sexuality that it is often very difficult to sort it all out without professional guidance.

These days it is not completely unusual to find people who have chosen celibacy for spiritual or social reasons. When this is the case, there are several choices to make about what to do with our sexuality and sexual energy. The obvious one is to shut ourselves down physically and sensually, which not only diminishes our sexuality, but also lowers our general sensitivity. The energy that we experience as a sexual feeling is really just a focusing of our basic vitality that unites with hormones and a primal instinctual momentum. This living force is what enables our connection to the living world around us. In time this suppression of a primary part of us lowers metabolism and the function of the immune system. It can even lower our neural functioning because we have told our body to "feel and be less." Some people come to relationships already sexually shut down, and choose specific partners for that reason.

In the spiritual traditions where there is a long history of retaining sexual energy, this process can go in several directions. There are several reasons for holding sexual energies. Since sexuality represents the release of vitality, the idea is to regulate it to the higher spiritual centers for spiritual development and to experience higher levels of consciousness. To achieve this end there are specific trainings and practices that often take years to master. There are other levels of celibacy in monastic traditions that are much less specific about what to do with these powerful energies. Often it is left to the renunciate to subsume it with devotion, hard work and love for others. But this direction often leads to physical stagnation, lethargy, and sometimes powerful and uncontrollable impulses that can harm others and create social difficulty (as the Catholic Church has so painfully found out).

In the history of the Asian medical traditions there is a specific literature pertaining to monk and nun diseases.

Most of it describes the physical result of too much sitting from meditation and prayer that can, after many years of inactivity, produce circulation problems in the legs as well as diabetes and issues with the reproductive system, bladder, and prostate. There are also references that include certain kinds of mania and unrestrained sexual impulses. With training and specific inner focus, meditative awareness and inner energetic techniques can move and shift the circulation and organ function to prevent most of these problems.

On the other side of the subject, there is a long and rich tradition of using the power of pleasure, bliss, and our sexuality for transformation and development. These techniques involve utilizing pleasure as a healing force to open constricted and traumatized areas to create a unified connection with the fundamental bliss of living. Many of you reading this may find this a lot more interesting and appealing than celibacy, but there are issues to pay attention to here as well.

Culturally, most of us have grown up with limited permission for pleasure and sensuality, but our body is clearly designed for these experiences. In most situations they are healing, renewing, and great for stress. In our youth, many of us engaged in serious experimentation and research in these areas, but as we get older our ability and interest in the intensity of these early experiences usually transitions so that pleasure and sexuality are a balanced and natural part of our life. But if we are thinking of using pleasure and sexuality for transformation, it is good to do so with awareness, allowing the language of our inner feelings and guidance to show us what is true and right for us.

The whole idea of liberation is to reach a state of openness, seeing clearly what is, living and acting between the polarity of attraction and resistance.

The lure of sexual pleasure can be a powerful force to simply dismiss. The trick is to maintain balance and awareness. So that just like when we have had one too many bites of ice cream and the sense of pleasure in the sweetness lessens the more we eat it, as we pay attention to our sensual experience, we may notice a diminishment in the level of sensory pleasure as our body becomes tired or depleted, or the importance of deeper intimacy and emotional connection begins to override the more physical aspects of the experience.

The whole idea of liberation is to reach a state of openness, seeing clearly what is, living and acting between the polarity of attraction and resistance.

As we get better at sensing what our body wants, we become increasingly adept at shifting the process of how it works and adapts in any given situation. For instance, if we're at a time in our life when there is not the opportunity for physical intimacy, we can learn to move our sexual energy from its normal concentration in the pelvis and genital area freely throughout our body, transforming it to energy and vitality. This doesn't have to warrant a sexual need for release, because rather than keeping it focused in one area we can let it fill us up as a vibrant energy that moves throughout our body.

Using sexuality for spiritual liberation is one of the most demanding tests of personal balance, concentration, and awareness. Allowing ourselves to be consumed by the powerful emergence of instinctual impulse and sensation while at the same time holding a subtle awareness of the transcendent experience of love that connects our physical experience to the highest reaches of consciousness may take just a little practice.

Love and Sex

Each of us has a unique sexual experience. Just as each of us might prefer chocolate or vanilla, each of us finds a certain personality and emotional configuration that is the sum total of who we are and where we've been up to the current moment. Our sexual preferences and styles also express our individuality. They are about reaching into areas that want expression, healing, closeness, and of course release. Let the awareness of pleasure and the pleasure of awareness guide you.

The union of love and sex has the potential to be the most powerful. There are of course other ways to meet. Sex and power, sex and submission, sex and aggression, even love and aggression and others—each of these represent the expression of different organ combinations: kidney/liver, heart/spleen, and so on. Love and sex represent the kidney and the heart: potentially the union and momentum of each stream of ancestors through the kidneys, with the mutual spiritual connections through the heart. When life and opportunity have allowed personality and transformative clarity to blossom, the union of love and sex can deepen into transcendence.

Deep Happy Inner Practice

Sensing Another

The central theme in any relationship is sensing the tone between the two of you.

How do you feel when you are in their presence?

Do you like yourself?

Do they like you? Respect and honor you?

Do you trust them?

Do you trust yourself with them?

Do you feel more or less like yourself when you are with them?

Do they drive you crazy?

Do they make you happy?

What do you like about them?

Who is answering these questions? Your head? Your heart? Your genitals? The lingering feelings evoked by the person that they remind you of?

It's important to know.

How still and quiet can you be with them?

Do they stimulate you? Intellectually? Spiritually? Emotionally? Sexually?

Do they make you close down a part of yourself?

Do they subtly make it difficult for you to tell them important things? Or to disagree with them?

Do you want to see them again but don't?

Do you not want to see them again but do anyway?

Is your relationship based on action, stillness, or just being?

Which do you prefer?

Do they help you to remember Deep Happy?

11

Let's Play Doctor—The Intelligence of Disease

To find nature herself, all her forms must be shattered.

—Meister Eckhart

One of the most important skills in Deep Happy is learning to be healthy. This kind of health is not only about being thin or radiant. It's about being deeply yourself, as a person and as a body. The messages that our bodies continually give us are as close to unneurotic truth as we will ever get in our physical world. We can only perceive them in the present moment. Our bodies are not present in the past, though remnants of past unprocessed experiences can reside there. Our bodies are a bridge to higher realms. Heart Math (*Heartmath.org*) research showed that the heart often has knowledge of coming events. Experiments by William Tiller showed that intuitive awareness of the future was not only possible, but common. Often these experiences are unacknowledged and attributed to hunches or luck. On this point it is important to keep in mind that this kind of intuitive experience is available most easily if we are picking up sensations and body messages in the present time.

It is vital to our personal development that we learn to understand this most ancient of body languages that is spoken to us with both tenderness and the abrupt alert of a heart attack. This chapter will have a more polarized tone than the rest of the book. There is much to think about here.

Most of what we know or think about disease in our culture is either wrong or greatly misunderstood. That may sound harsh to say, but the majority of us have been brainwashed into not trusting our bodies. We have been taught in schools, from our medical doctors, from television specials and articles in newspapers and magazines, and well-meaning parents that disease is something that attacks us—that it is only bad. We have wars on cancer. We have national alerts concerning impending and dubious flus and we are bombarded with television ads warning us to go to the hospital if our medication-induced erection lasts more than four hours.

I have tried to keep from being very political in this book, but on this topic I have to speak out. Our conventional attitudes and teachings about health care are myths told by the profit-driven drug companies, hospitals, and medical providers more interested in making a buck than understanding the deeper nature of disease and raising the quality of people's lives. This is a shame and embarrassment to science and to the long tradition of medicine and healing. Although there is decisive evidence concerning corporate fraud and malfeasance, the system has made it all but impossible for most well-meaning physicians to either investigate other paradigms or implement new ideas, treatments, and strategies.

Even well-educated people with knowledge of holistic and natural medicine often run for antibiotics at the first sign of a fever or cold, not even realizing their negative effects or that there are safe and more effective natural alternatives that are easily available. Unlearning our ingrained beliefs takes time, as does getting used to the idea that there is no Santa Claus. This is especially true for well-meaning parents when there is so much pressure from other parents, school health programs, and the media. These attitudes are in direct contradiction to huge amounts of existing research, though much of it has been misrepresented by the pharmaceutical companies in collusion with academia, and the massive health provider networks.

For example, in 1978 researchers at the University of Michigan found that fever was beneficial; if it was monitored and allowed its natural course, patients would get well sooner and stay well much longer than if their fevers were suppressed with antibiotics or other methods. No major hospital in the United States has paid any attention to this research. It is common knowledge that antibiotics have no effect on viruses, and in fact weaken our immune systems at a time when we most need them. Antibiotics slow down or stop the function of our immune reaction which will then have the appearance of reducing fever and inflammation. This may sound like the right effect, but in fact this suppression of our immune response just shoves toxins or biological pathogens deeper into our bodies.

Alexander Fleming invented penicillin in 1928, but within a few years he was warning fellow doctors about its use. This initial use of antibiotics created an economic surge that marked the beginning of one of the most powerful lobbies; it financed the eventual near demise of the homeopathic and naturopathic movements in the United States. The misuse of "quick-fix" antibiotics has created a worldwide epidemic of biological resistance.

It is fair to say that antibiotics initially allowed the successful treatment of many previously difficult to treat diseases, including pneumonia and syphilis. They also created greater resources in public health. No one can be blamed for jumping on the antibiotics bandwagon. Over time, as the side effects and long-term effects began to show, very little was done in the way of considering alternative treatments. In Germany, France, and other developed countries, new and groundbreaking methods were researched, developed, and incorporated into the medical profession. Homeopathy is a medical specialty in France, and Germany developed very interesting diagnostic and therapeutic devices starting in the 1950s. These took Eastern approaches and new developments in physics into the arms of modern science. These devices, although therapeutically proven, are currently resisted by the FDA. In Europe now, Big Pharma is pushing to outlaw the public availability of many herbs and supplements, even though Phyto-medicine or herbology has been used by all the cultures of the world since we wore animal skins and hunted with stone clubs.

Fortunately, this information is now coming to the light. One book that explores these themes is *The Truth*

About the Drug Companies: How They Deceive Us and What to Do About It by Marcia Angell, a senior lecturer in social medicine at Harvard Medical School and former editor in chief of *The New England Journal of Medicine*. The power of the pharmaceutical companies and medical lobbies has driven and skewed the philosophy of health—not just with financially motivated propaganda, but much more seriously and illegally with deceptive and misrepresented research that has put the lives of millions in jeopardy and exponentially added to the huge economic burden of our national health care policies, which themselves need serious healing and loving attention.

The effects of stepping beyond the natural intelligence of our million-plus years of biological momentum can be surprising. In the last chapter I mentioned the effect that antibiotics had on confusing the mating choices of fruit flies. Who would have guessed that such a seemingly random influence as antibiotics could radically shift the mating choices of an entire species?

I am not against antibiotics or medicine per se—it is just that deeper effects of the overall policies of the pharmaceutical industry have created more harm than good. We must take time to understand them, looking from a wide and unbiased perspective, making use of them if absolutely necessary, with full knowledge of their long-range effects and after full consideration of safer and more economical alternatives.

I have been practicing natural medicine for forty years. I've worked at clinics in California, Massachusetts, Illinois, Taiwan, China, Tibet, Hong Kong, and Nepal.

My studies have included extensive training in Chinese medicine, biomedical sciences, acupuncture, several systems of herbal medicine, Qigong and energetic healing, homeopathy, nutritional medicine, biofeedback, neurofeedback, many kinds of massage and bodywork, several kinds of cranial work, and many other therapeutic modalities. I have worked with psychiatrists, internists, orthopedists, sports medicine specialists, chiropractors, midwives, and biological dentists. I have studied everything I could find in current developments in Western physiology, neurophysiology, and the energetic systems of every form of Eastern medicine. I mention all this not because I'm so great—there is still so much I don't know or haven't yet integrated. But I do know that…

There is an intelligence to disease!

So much of modern research has been conducted under the assumption that disease is the end result of mistakes that the body makes. In fact, on a micro level, the body does seem to get in its own way at times, especially at the cellular and neurological level. But if we were to consider all the systemic interactions as having a purpose, then whatever pathology we are looking at makes more sense. On a macro level, where we look at most disease as a multi-system event, it is often much easier to understand the intelligence of the process—in other words, what the body is trying to accomplish.

When you think about it, it makes sense that fever is good for us. The elevated body temperature kills bacteria, changes pH, stimulates the immune system, discharges poisons from the body, and releases suppressed emotional material. Having a fever takes more time than getting rid of it with a pill, like sweeping dirt under the rug. Usually when we get a cold or flu, it happens at a time when we need rest, space, and perspective to pay attention to something else that is going on in our lives.

I have worked with chronic headache patients for over thirty years. The vast majority of them had a gap between who they really were and the persona that they showed the world. For most of them, the headache signaled a departure from the truth of who they knew themselves to be. As they identified their more authentic voice and became able to express themselves, the headaches got better, sometimes on the spot. I found this to be true even with migraines.

Childhood diseases like mumps, measles, and chickenpox have been normal part of our culture for many centuries. Babies and young children have a great deal of energy. They fall down, get up, run around, get lots of little infections and diseases, and are generally fine. In Eastern medicine we know this essential energy is important for the children to keep them safe and strong so their bodies can learn to both play and adapt to local pathogens. (Children who are kept too clean and germ free by nervous parents have higher rates of illness.) Generally, childhood diseases are about the release of heat from the core of the body. Mumps, measles, chickenpox, and so forth are all about relieving this extra energy from the core of children. These diseases happen to them about the time they're learning to be quiet and still in school. Most childhood diseases are part of our normal and healthy developmental experience. Yet, currently as we eliminate them the learning difficulties, anxiety, ADD and ADHD are on the rise. Could it be that by not allowing the natural release of this developmental energy we are causing healthy but sensitive kids to go a little crazy—like too much heat in a pressure cooker?

There are several factors that cause us to ignore the intelligence of disease. The most prevalent is the prevailing misunderstanding that symptoms of any kind are always bad. Our culture teaches us not to trust what the body tells us through body sensations and physical symptoms. It is also surprisingly common for people to not consider that an uncomfortable sensation after eating might be from eating something that the body doesn't like. Many of us take antacids or digestive enzymes after eating rather than taking time to notice that we may have intolerances to certain foods like wheat, potatoes, or dairy products. In actuality, many more people suffer from deficient stomach acid and their conditions are exacerbated by antacids, resulting in gastric numbness rather than healing. Likewise, many people complain of not having enough energy and choose to take medicine instead of getting more sleep, eating better, noticing what they're worrying about, or even just putting more fun in their lives. On a certain level, there are many herbs and natural supplements that can make you feel like you have more energy, but although these can be helpful, we have to make sure that our deeper reserves are replenished so as to avoid deeper deficits.

These days we rush to the doctor for a quick fix when our children come down with rashes and fevers instead of doing what our grandparents did—put us to bed for a few days with lots of fluids. The primary cause of this misunderstanding of childhood diseases is the promotion of vaccines by the pharmaceutical industry.

This is not to say that the illnesses of children shouldn't be carefully monitored, especially in babies and little children. Treating children is an important specialty, but these days there are also many excellent naturopaths, Oriental medical practitioners, and holistic physicians trained with effective natural therapies and medicines. These therapies are safe and well researched, without the toxic side effects.

The therapies we use in integrative clinics for kids with learning, mood, and behavior issues are without the long-term negative or even addicting effects on personality and self-esteem that are common when taking most prescription medicine. One of the great tragedies of our modern culture is the medicating of our children for behavior and emotional patterns, especially in the areas of depression, ADHD, and the new highly promoted diagnosis of bipolar disorder. These so-called diseases are very commonly misdiagnosed and can often be resolved over time with diet, natural medicines, recognition of stress patterns, and parent and teacher reeducation. Acupuncture, homeopathy, some forms of chiropractics, cranial realignment, herbs and nutritional supplements, and neurofeedback when administered by trained and experienced experts can also be extremely useful. In most instances they create systemic health and balance rather than psychological dependence and dangerous side effects that weaken young bodies and alter developing personalities.

Is it any wonder that the major mortal illness of women is heart disease? Isn't it women who carry the heart of any society? In our modern world the qualities of the heart—love, the power of vulnerability, and compassion—are so often diminished in favor of drive, intensity, emotional restraint, and denial. No wonder women's hearts are susceptible to coronary disease.

The hallmark of the paradigm we are working toward, which is actually an ancient paradigm, is that consciousness creates biology. How we think and feel creates our bodies. This is directly opposite to contemporary views on modern neuroscience that posit that consciousness is an incidental by-product of biology. The great American-born Canadian neuroscientist Wilder Penfield had a more creative differing view:

"The form of that energy (mind) is different from that of neuronal potentials that travel the axon pathways. There I must leave it."

After an esteemed lifetime of investigating the brain, Wilder Penfield came to the conclusion that mind could not be found in the brain—that consciousness and physical form were independent of each other and that the structures of the brain allowed the mind to be perceived and utilized. This was a profound conclusion coming from a scientist.

Throughout history many of the greatest scientists professed and were inspired by mystical insights. From the early Chinese physician Hwa To up through Pythagoras, Isaac Newton, Einstein, and Niels Bohr, the great discoveries have come through widening the accepted vistas of thought and social custom.

The universe is speaking to us every instant on every channel.

Our continuous connection to and direct awareness of the *big* reality influences our thoughts and feelings and subtly shifts our bodies and DNA on a moment to moment basis. Ideas and revamped perspectives are constantly shooting through the brain and nervous system, continually revamping old and constructing new neural and energetic pathways.

I think we've all had the experience of feeling stressed and then caught sight of ourselves, relaxed for a moment, and then felt better. This is a very simple example, but the same process works for many complicated situations. Perhaps we feel an ache or a pain in the pit of our stomach. If we just relax and gently breathe in, noticing how the feeling changes as the inhale breath expands the area and the exhale relaxes it, we will probably notice that with each breath we begin to feel better and better. It may take a few minutes to get the hang of it. Don't be impatient. I have used the same method in a much more detailed form to help clients with very serious diseases, in some cases even cancer. *An important point:* when working with serious medical, physical, or emotional problems, make sure that you contact an experienced medical person.

The universe is speaking to us every instant on every channel.

It is true that we all have the ability to heal ourselves from even very serious conditions, but we also all have the *very popular* ability to mislead ourselves about something that might be difficult for us to accept or even more importantly, that we want to believe. So please take an optimistic but realistic look at things and get second opinions from knowledgeable people. It is also unlikely that your regular physician will have any idea about your ability to self-heal, and probably won't understand what you're talking about. It may take a little time to find someone with both the medical experience and perspective to be of help here, but persevere. Begin trying it on little things: aches and pains, digestive sensations, fatigue, menstrual cramps, stress and tension, even low back pain. Experiment!

Deep Happy Inner Practice

After settling yourself, try breathing into the area that hurts or feels poorly.

Notice how the focused expansion and release of the breath feels there.

Take time; be curious about what is happening and what it feels like.

Let the inhale bring in a nourishing energy, and let the exhale relax you more deeply and carry away pain, toxicity, and old emotional imprints. You may be surprised that most things change with just a little time. I have used this to literally save my life several times and taught it to thousands of others; it really works.

Deep Happy Inner Practice

Finding the Intelligence of Illness

The next time you get a cold or a sore back or neck, ask yourself this question: What have I missed? Is there something that I have been pushing away? Some feeling or awareness that I have been avoiding?

Are you more tired than you have let yourself realize? Have you not given yourself permission or time that you need to catch up to yourself?

The next time you get a bladder infection, ask yourself: What is going on with my intimate relationship?

The next time you run for aspirin or antibiotics to put down a fever, ask yourself: If fever is not a good thing, why is my body producing it? Perhaps you could try seeking help with a practitioner or physician who will work with your body's intelligence and help you to understand the message that it is trying to tell you.

Ask yourself this question: Do I trust my body? If you don't, think about what voices or influences brought you to that way of thinking. Is there anything about the will and intelligence of your body that you do trust?

These are just a few ideas; there are many ways to delve into this. Be creative—your well-being, health, and even sanity are at stake. Your Deep Happy does not necessarily depend on a happy body, but happy bodies make life much easier.

12

Karma

You to Buddha, no distance. Karma to no karma, try awareness, and acceptance.

—Bodhidharma

Like gravity, karma is so basic we often don't even notice it.

—Sakyong Mipham

KARMA IS ANOTHER ONE of those things that everyone has something to say about, but few seem to think it through. First of all, there are those who think karma is about blame and punishment. This sounds like old-time religion to me-the methods and fear-based strategies designed to control simple minds and simple hearts. Karma is not like that.

I do not believe in a vindictive karma, universe, God, or any higher power. It doesn't make sense to me and it doesn't follow anything I've learned about the nature of reality.

For one thing, I've never met a vindictive person who had wisdom and compassion or was deeply happy. As I wrote about earlier, the bad things people do can be traced back to aberrations in their physiology from trauma, negative imprinting, and patterns from other times. If the universe or God is our parent, why in the world would he or she blame me for a mistake or misunderstanding?

Karma also has a Buddha Nature.

When my son was three years old and broke something or called me a boo-boo head, I didn't denounce him as evil. I simply remembered that he was only three and hadn't figured it all out yet, noticed if he was tired or hungry or didn't understand something, and did my best to love him. We aren't any different than my three-year-old.

We are always doing our best at each moment, even when that is very hard to believe. Why would we be punished by karma or any other force in the universe for making a mistake? The whole of creation would have vanished long ago if that were the case. Polarity and retribution are unstable and unsustainable in the long run.

I think the best way to talk about karma is to talk about love. In this regard, I don't mean the love of things or the love that can be more or less love. I'm speaking of infinite love—love in the sense of non-duality, well beyond the confines of description, although I guess that's what we are trying to do here. In this sense, it is love as the field of pure awareness; it is life itself in everything. It may be that we are doing the word "love" a disservice. After all it is a word that has been so used and misused for every imaginable thing or occasion. It must have lost its meaning by now? But that's the thing about love—there's no place it can't go

Karma also has a Buddha Nature.

and there's nothing that it isn't. No matter how much we use it, it's still love.

Love is certainly not vindictive, nor is it jealous, or vain, or unwilling. It is only the illusion of the absence of love that holds these attitudes of separation.

So how does love (karma) work? It only seeks union and balance. There is nothing that could ever be in its way. Since it is the pervasive connection among all things beyond time and space, it senses tension and disconnection and can always tell when we, as a resolving point of awareness, are on the wrong track. Its only purpose is to awaken us back—first into the perception of union, then to the direct experience beyond union. It nudges us in the gentlest of ways. If we miss that first look love gives us, we can count on it to persevere. Rest assured that love/karma will keep at it until it finally gets our attention. Sometimes this is stubbing our toe because we are angry or upset and not paying attention and sometimes this means getting cancer or being hit by a semi while trying to change a tire along Highway 101.

Again, this force could not be here to punish us for not knowing. It is just love, caring so much that the thought of temporary discomfort or even losing our body is nothing compared to separation from our connection to the timeless everything. Punishment only creates separation, not the clarity needed to change or heal. In this way love/karma is neutral—it only seeks balance.

I have always understood karma to be like a guitar string, gradually letting go of its twang, slowly settling, seeking a renewed balance in stillness, yet always ready to play along with Coltrane or to hum the tune of a comet all of its own accord.

How could there be "bad karma"?

In the huge scale of things, there is only the karma that awakens. It works its way in somewhere between the gentlest and toughest love. Whatever we need, whatever we can handle. Not too shabby!

Karma is the love of creation tending its flock.

Oh, and one more thing: What about building up a reservoir of good karma through service or spiritual practice? Read this story, make up your own mind.

Recently I heard about research being done in Japan by Hiroshi Motoyama, the world famous Shinto mystic and scientist. He was researching the effects of distant healing in his laboratory on E. coli bacteria that had been deliberately injured by heat. There was one strain that was just not responding to the healings. Somewhere in the middle of the experiments, one of his lab assistants got an idea. They called a local charity and donated money in the name of that bacteria strain. From that moment on, the calculated results of the research showed very specific improvements in the healing of the E. coli. The explanation from his lab was that adding positive actions in the name of the bacteria increased its good karma. Writing this it occurred to me that it might have instead added positive energy to the karmic stream of the researchers. No matter which version you choose, good actions and intent = good!

Karma is the love of creation tending its flock.

Deep Happy Inner Practice

Opening to Karma

Whenever you are confronted with a difficult situation, a recurring troubling theme in your life, or a sudden shift in your plans, ask yourself this question: If this is about being loved and awakened by the universe, which I am intimately a part of, then what is the meaning of what is happening to me?

What am I missing?
What do I need to learn?
What is the blessing?
Drop into the stillness,
let the answer come
let it dissolve . . .
again and again and again . . .

13

Breathing Nature

Silence is the closest thing to God.

—Meister Eckhart

WE *ARE* NATURE.

No matter how much the tumor between our ears tries to convince us otherwise, we, us, man, woman, people, humans, are not separate and special (though we are each unique) from the rest of life. In the end, the truth is this: We are really not too different from tree frogs, orangutans, and flounder. I know those of you with a pro-human bias might complain (it's good to be species supportive), but all of us species are the result of an infinite number of biological and conscious lineages whose ancestry extends back beyond time and probably even knowing. That is the most profound wonder of it all.

In so many inexplicable ways, the birds, bees, flowers, trees, minerals, volcanoes, giant squid, viruses, bacteria, and everything else imaginable are our family. We have all arisen out of the primordial quantum electromagnetic plasma pond of possibility. Whether you believe that we were made by the breath of God or that we are the result of an infinite chain of developing genetic possibilities, no one can argue that, at least on a biological and relative world level, we didn't make ourselves. All life is interconnected. There are hundreds of billions if not trillions of other life forms living in, on, and around our bodies all the time. Even the most basic of our energy sources, mitochondria, are symbiotic parasites that come with a very different stream of DNA than our own. It's basically the "I'll scratch your back if you scratch mine" idea that works in just about every cell in our body.

The elements of the earth are also the earth of our bodies. If that is not enough to think about, our blood is basically sea water with a dash of hemoglobin. Exactly the same elements and components that make our world make us. It is really very hard to find anything about us that is that different from anyone or any thing else.

"But humans make things, don't they?" you might ask. Well, so do beavers, ants, bees, spiders, and many other species. Plants make rutabagas, almonds, curare, and medicines for every ailment. All species make something. Just as we raise squab and collect caviar, so do ants raise aphids for food.

What about computers? Yes, we humans make computers, but they are substandard compared what is between our ears. And compared to the petite pea-sized brain in my African gray parrot, Sophie, who is smarter than any German Shepherd and can *talk(!)*, the CPU in my MacBook Pro seems pretty bulky. All life and consciousness contributes to the whole. We are each like the cells of our body. Some of us are cells from the frontal cortex of the brain, or liver cells, or glia. It would be easy to say that one cell is more important than another, but our body needs us all and will replace us when the time comes for our consciousness to let go of our worn out physical form and we get to try another body in another reality.

This afternoon, just before I started to write this chapter, I walked outside to take my son, Namkai, to a friend's house. We live on a thousand-foot hill in Marin County, surrounded by trees, plants, and sky overlooking all of San Francisco Bay. It is late February and the rain has been steadily coming down all day. The plants are in their prime. The smell is both invigorating and relaxing at the same time. But this afternoon, walking up the steps through the many plants, it occurred to me to try to smell each little fragrance that made up the whole at the same time. I had never tried to do that before, and it was like listening to all the individual instruments in a symphony, while at the same time taking in the entirety of the music.

Just walking up those stairs in that open and receptive state reminded me of all the individual plants that surround us and add to our lives. Each plant gives off a unique scent and energy if we can get still enough to sense it. Many plants have subtle but direct influences on our bodies.

We take specific herbal teas for various things. Mint cools us down and may help certain headaches; ginger has a warming effect and may help certain issues of digestion; and so forth. There are over twenty thousand clinically useful herbs in the traditional Chinese materia medica, and thousands more that are part of the other Asian, European, and North American herbal systems. We are just beginning to fully discover the treasure of botanical substances in the Amazon.

We may not even have to take the physical part of the plant into our body. The fragrance and energy signature or tone of the plant may be enough to help our systems shift into a higher state of function. If we just stand or sit in the presence of an individual or group of plants, smelling them, letting our eyes and senses take them in, we may be able to detect subtle but specific effects. You may notice these effects right away or it may take a little time for you to feel them, but this is a real and normal ability and experience that our bodies are designed for and waiting to have. As I said at the beginning of this chapter, we are nature. The plants are part of our family, too.

Deep Happy Inner Practice

Breathing Nature

As you feel and breathe in the fragrance and essence of a plant, notice how it makes you feel and if or how it changes your body or mental state. Can you feel a sensation in any particular place in your body—perhaps your shoulders, your liver, or your skin? Do you feel more awake or relaxed? Do you feel an itchy sensation or tingling? Or maybe what you experience is difficult to put into words, but you know something very real and specific is affecting you.

With a little practice you can become very adept at this kind of sensing. Your body's ability to pick up all these sensations and energies will most likely surprise you, but with a little prodding your body and energy systems will begin to present you with new and interesting experiences.

On a less subtle level, we have all been affected by being in the presence of someone, even without directly interacting with them. They might be depressed and bring down our mood. Or we might have felt the delightful effects of being around people who were happy, positive, self-assured, inspired, and contagiously interactive. This is exactly the same phenomenon as sensing the various energies of nature. Even in our constructed world we can sense how a house, building, or area feels. We are designed for these activities. When we are in survival situations, our many latent abilities come out again. I have talked with a number of soldiers who have reported that very quickly after first moving into a combat zone, they find that they often get a sense of impending danger or of changing situations. It seems that the soldiers who survive year after year are most proficient at this kind of heightened sensitivity.

It is not just in the areas of survival that we can uncover other latent abilities. These same abilities come into play when we meditate or tune in to higher or wider states of awareness. If we have been used to eating highly spiced food and all of a sudden we are served very simple food one night for dinner, our first impression might be that the food seems tasteless. As we begin to chew and relax our preconceptions about what we first expect, a whole world of previously unnoticed flavors can arise. We might even notice that the brown rice we are chewing has five unique flavors that appear in succession.

Deep Happy Inner Practice

Experiencing the Earth and Direction

Walk into the woods, a garden, or a natural area.

Find a place where you want to stand and close your eyes.

Slowly turn in a circle.

See if you can feel differences in your body and mood depending on which direction you are facing. There are 360 degrees in a circle; there will be at least that many subtle variations in how you feel as you turn. As we sequentially face the main compass directions of East, South, West, and North, our body will probably sense the biggest differences.

Which direction feels the best?

Is there a direction that doesn't feel as good?

With practice you can learn to sense which way you are facing by the feel of it.

Next, sense what the land or rock beneath your feet feels like. Just like sensing the energy of plants or which direction you are facing, you can easily learn to distinguish the structures and elemental energies in the ground. This is easier to than you might think.

We all have this innate ability and can easily learn to access it.

Once I visited the home of a friend who had a mineral collection in a glass case in his living room. There were over eighty little spheres, each made of a different substance. We decided to do an experiment. I went into a standing meditative posture and internal state. Then, one by one, my friend put a different mineral in my hand. With each one my body went into a different and spontaneous movement. Rocking, swaying, shaking, wiggling, and so forth, I never would have thought that I would be able to come up with so many different variations. I just let it happen, watching as my body generated each new movement seemingly on its own. We went through thirty minerals and as many different spontaneous movements. This is a very surprising example of how our bodies have many mostly unused abilities. Not only could my body and energetic systems clearly indentify the individual properties and frequencies of each substance, but also it could also create movements that represented them. In my own experiences training physicians and lay people, I have been continually amazed at the human body's ability to sense the subtlest of the infinite details of the world around us.

Deep Happy Inner Practice

The Experience of Nature

Stand on the ground anywhere, especially in a natural environment.

Let your preconceptions and expectations fall away. Just relax and be present.

Open your awareness to everything around you.

Notice any smells or sounds or sensations, like the sun or breeze as they warm or cool your body. Take a few deep breaths and let them out slowly.

Continued

Feel exactly what it feels like when the breath comes in and when it goes out.

Relax your body. If there are areas that won't relax, notice them and let it be okay for them to be as they are.

Let your mind become quiet and calm; if this is difficult, notice the thoughts and let that be okay as well. See if you can experience the three-dimensional space of your head or body and where the thoughts and feelings are coming from. Can you feel any sensations within the three-dimensional spaces anywhere in your body?

Now try sensing the tone and quality of the energy of the location you are in. How would you describe it?

Try sensing/feeling the tone and energetic personality of the various plants around you.

If you are in the desert, all the energy that is tied up in the plants is free in the air. Can you feel differences as you move around?

Rocks and minerals each have a different tone and vibration. Over the next few months, let yourself become familiar with participating in the natural world at this level of awareness and sensitivity.

The important point is to have fun with this. Enjoy the wonders of our natural abilities.

This kind of sensing is a little different for everyone and takes different amounts of time for each person to get used to. Some feel, some hear, some smell, and so forth. As you develop increasing sensitivity and you get better and clearer on the subtle difference, doubt and distraction fall away!

Eventually you will become used to being like this all the time, even in very stimulating environments like large crowds. Your system will also adjust your level of sensitivity to whatever is comfortable, while at the same time bringing certain bits of relevant information to your attention automatically. Deep Happy.

Deep Happy Inner Practice

Feeling Beneath the Earth

Close your eyes and notice the tone or frequency of the ground beneath your feet.

What does it feel like? How firm or soft does it feel?

Does it have a pleasant or uncomfortable feeling to it?

Does the ground feel moist or dry? Try sensing what the feeling and energy feels like one foot below you, then five feet, then ten, twenty, and so on. Can you feel variations in density for different layers or even pools of water or accumulations of particular minerals?

You will be surprised at how much you can perceive.

Speaking to Nature

Another very interesting and enlightening thing to try is learning to listen to and speak with the spirit of individual sources of nature. The essential essence of mountains, species, plants, and areas can all be talked to and learned from. I remember driving through the higher part of Rocky Mountain National Park. I got a strong feeling that I needed to stop the car at a certain place, hike out to a high plateau, find the right spot, and listen, so that is what I did. This may sound crazy, but there is little or no downside. Whether it's just your imagination or something real, find out! The upside is profound.

I got out of the car and scanned with my eyes while at the same time feeling each location that my eyes looked at. Within a minute I knew where to go. It took about twenty minutes to walk up and over to where I felt like I was being guided to go. As I walked in that direction I kept checking in, just like looking at a compass while hiking, to the feeling that was guiding me. When I arrived at the area, I couldn't feel anything at first; my rational mind began to think I had made a mistake, but within a few moments I got very clear guidance to move to a spot about twenty feet from where I was and to face a certain direction, then stand still and be quiet. Sometimes these inner directions come as a very distinct voice, and other times it's something else—a feeling—but one that has a kind if implied non-verbal and directional perception to it.

There I was, standing at perhaps fourteen thousand feet in a deserted and cold field, opening myself to the spirit of the mountain. And then it spoke to me in an inner voice that was so peaceful and resonant that I never could have imagined it or made it up. My whole being entrained with the inner sound of it.

The voice of the mountain told me what I needed to know for the next phase of my research and personal development. Its vibration was more helpful than the words that were spoken to me, because the feeling of them shifted something inside of me that made moving into my next step more possible. It lasted a few minutes and I said out loud, "Thank you," and walked back to some rocks and sat down for a while. I wasn't able to think—it would not have been possible for me. I just sat there in the cold stillness of the Rockies, feeling pretty good.

Each of us will have our own version of this experience, because each of us listens differently. Each source that we speak to will have a unique way of conveying its message to us. Several years ago while visiting my mother and stepdad in Florida, I had the opportunity to spend some time way out in the country on a large tract of untouched, pristine land. I spent several hours sitting and walking through the area tuning into the plants and elemental energies. Finally, while resting on a rock in the sunlight that trickled through the lush green foliage, I decided to speak to the essence of the forest. The voice that came back was very unusual in my experience of these things. It sounded humorous and profound at the same time, and as it spoke I could feel the combined essence of the local botanical community. It was surprisingly welcoming and polite, and asked me to carry the memory and vibration with me wherever I went. The voice thanked me for letting it feel and incorporate the vibrational memories of the various places on the earth that I carried with me into its local understanding of the planet. This was surprising to me; I would not have thought about it like that. It especially liked the memories of the tropical areas where I had been: South East Asia, India, and Central America were similar in climate, but very different ecologically. It was a surprising juxtaposition for me to find such a refined essence in the spirit of the land and plants of Florida when compared to the overall cultural milieu there.

It is also possible to talk to the consciousness of a species. About four years ago I was walking down a driveway in Novato, California, a town not far from where I was living at the time. It was a hot, sunny afternoon with just a touch of a cool breeze that had made its way over the hill from the ocean. I had just received a very deep energy healing session from a friend who was a powerful Iranian healer. I was definitely in an altered and aware state. His house was on the top of a hill that looked out over the surrounding area. It was my custom to park my car a ways away so I that I could have some reentry time before driving and also because the area was so beautiful.

I looked out over a grassy valley of open land down below. At the bottom to my right were a small growth of low trees and some bushes surrounding a tiny pond. There were frogs croaking, and I had the idea to sit on the side of the hill to listen to them. After about ten minutes of this, it occurred to me to see if I could communicate to the over spirit of them, to their combined consciousness. I have been concerned about diminishing frog populations in many areas of the world. So I sat there with my eyes open in a meditative and open state and simply directed my consciousness down toward the sound of the frogs coming from the pond. I sensed them as a whole, tuning in to what I perceived as their combined personality.

Within a few moments the frog spirit spoke to me plainly and sincerely. It told me that the sound of their croaking was designed to carry the vibrational essence of the water with the specific local minerals that the water had absorbed out to the surrounding area, spreading its nourishing energetic signature. When I expressed my concern about the future of the world's frogs and told of how dear they were to the people of the earth (I tried not to think of the French passion for frog legs), the frog voice answered very lovingly that they were okay and were just receding quietly for a while, waiting for certain energies to pass as they inevitably would. It then thanked me and asked me to remember our connection.

The final story in this chapter is the most important for this book because it is what helped it come about. After having my proposal for Deep Happy accepted and receiving the initial check from my publisher, my creative process stopped in its tracks. For six weeks my mind went back and forth with ideas and chapter possibilities. My inner neurotic self rejected everything as not being good enough or profound enough. I began to worry that I might not write the book at all.

One morning I decided to take the dogs for a walk. We live at the top of one of the highest hills in Marin County, right next to a hundred square miles of open land, woods, and coastal mountains. From our house we can walk on a high ridge where on one side we can see all of San Francisco Bay and on the other the beautiful hills with hints of the ocean beyond. About a half mile down the trail, it curves to the right and there in front of you is Mount Tamalpais, in all its majestic glory.

Many years ago I had a client who was a psychic and channel and he suggested talking to the spirit of Mount

Tam. I tried it and received some interesting guidance. So that sunny morning with my happy dogs urging me to keep walking, I stopped and bowed to the mountain. My hands were pressed together in front of my heart, and with the deepest humility I could muster, I asked, "What do I need to know to write my book?"

After a very short pause and in what sounded like the deep voice of Moses, I heard, "It's not the Bible!" I burst out laughing, my three dogs cocking their heads at me as only dogs can do.

That moment released all my obsessive caution about what to write. I bowed again and thanked the mountain for the slap in the heart that woke me up. The next morning I began to write, and continued until I was finished.

If you have not had experiences like this, they might seem kind of "out there," but keep in mind that they tend to have an aura of normalcy about them when they are happening. The great consciousness of all minds of the many realms is speaking to us all the time. We might not always be aware of it, but in truth our seemingly singular insights into our intricate and wondrous universe may indeed be gifts from unseen benefactors.

Deep Happy Inner Practice

Listening to the Consciousness of Nature

When the feeling inspires you, try speaking with the consciousness or spirit of an individual species or source of land. Be open and humble; don't worry about being ceremonial or serious. Just be you.

Ask or speak from your heart, then listen. Don't be surprised if the answer is simple or even funny. Let what you hear touch you, and the resonance will let you know the reality of it. You are making big friends here. Enjoy them!

14

Death and Beyond

Death is safe.

—Ram Dass

IT MAY SEEM ODD to include a chapter on death in a book about being happy, yet death is something we will all have to face. It is the tyrannosaurus in the room. Whether it will surprise us suddenly as we finish reading this sentence or come in slow expectation when we are old and bedridden, it is a reality that lurks in the back of the minds of all those who take time to think about it.

I am always surprised when I feel afraid of death. For years, I puzzled over it. I have had many transcendental, non-body, meditative, and chemical experiences, so it was surprising that sometimes, late at night, I could have a moment of cold terror thinking about my impending death. Then one night I came to understand it.

Death is the great solvent. It dissolves our bodies and all the things about us—all but our most essential nature and our innate awareness. Death is so complete that the mere thought of it pries loose the doors and openings that guard us from the deepest and most primal of our inner voices. The awareness of death is in our software. It works behind the scenes, preparing us if we let it, getting us used to the idea, so that optimally, as in the sacred traditions, we can meet our death with openness, awareness, and maybe even joy. But most of us have work to do if we are to be there in sacred readiness, curious as to where the next stop on our journey will take us.

Curiosity brings its own courage.

We all have this voice of fear within us. It is the fundamental survival program of the body. It is there to keep our body safe and is a very good thing. The bigger perspective includes also remembering to experience part of us that is untouched by our bodies and the world. Then our fear becomes a welcome reminder to pay attention to the transient beauty of life and not an obstruction of the simple joy of being alive in the multi-verse of our existence. Since I first came to understand this process, I have watched with interest whenever the fear of death grips me. Holding the process in this neutral and curious way focuses the experience of fear as a direct and somatic unfolding within me. If I pay close attention, I can notice the fear in my body as a sensation. When we notice these body sensations as a separate physical stimulus, the patterns of fear become manageable. Fear is just my body realizing its mortality, and has little to do with the continuous presence of being that is both deathless and timeless.

Curiosity brings its own courage.

While living in Nepal, I noticed this dichotomy of physical and energetic individuation. Meditators and yogis coming out of long retreat could still have unhealed personalities, and yet the energetic core of their consciousness would be shimmering and radiant, apparent to anyone in their presence. The body and the collective consciousness of its parts and ancestry are different from the consciousness of our inner being. Our fear of death is of the body. The joyous and fearless anticipation of our eventual transition comes as we learn to trust, experiment with, and test our connection to this inner part of us. The gradual integration of this vast awareness comes through the portal of our spiritual heart. As we learn to live from there, it becomes a channel for direct knowledge, guidance, and nourishment. In time, the post-traumatic patterns that cause us to be out of sync with the physical and energetic systems of the body can be healed, and we find increasing familiarity with the inner part of us that is in continual deep union with the infinite. This is toward enlightenment.

We can also think our way through the fear of losing our bodies and the process of dying. We all remember our last life and know well our previous body. We were upside down in fluid, in the mostly dark, breathing through our tummies, experiencing our life through sound, vibration, feelings, and the chemicals running through our mother's bloodstream. We were directly connected to the consciousness of our mothers, fathers, and the timeless universe. For the most part we were happy and eager; our days and nights were spent in biological and energetic adaptation and connection, preparing for our next life—this one. We could feel and express love and fear and we knew the voices and the lives of those beyond the skin wall where we lived and could communicate with them physically and emotionally.

Then one day strange sensations began to occur. We may have felt excitement and anxiety. Suddenly, propelled against our will out of our warm, safe, and familiar world, we were moved headfirst through a very tight and confining tunnel and into the light. Hallelujah, rebirth!

And there we were, in a new world, in a new body. Perhaps even held and loved by those whom we had heard, communicated with, and felt, but whom we had never actually seen or touched. We survived, maybe even prospered. It turned out okay. After all, here you are reading this!

So, the next question is: Where were you before that? You must have been somewhere. Yet here we are, two lives later and probably still okay. Where were we?

My mother was funny, creative, and dramatic. One morning when she was in her late eighties, she was cutting fruit in her kitchen when she slipped, accidentally pushing a knife into her throat as she fell to the floor. We later found out that she had a stroke. She was medivacced to the hospital, where doctors repaired the wound in her neck and thought she would recover after several months of rehab. Several days later she went into a coma. A brain scan revealed that she had many small strokes before her recent one, and that there was very little left of her brain. After much consultation, we decided to disconnect life support.

When I first called on the day of my mother's admission, the attending nurse suggested that I not come to visit right away because she would need me during rehab. Then my mother surprised everyone by going into a coma, and I did not get to be with her in person during her last few days.

Without food, nourishment or added oxygen, she lasted for five days. She was always stubborn. Several times each day, from California, I would go into meditation and talk to her. For the first four days she was still in her personality, wondering what was going on, even asking where she was or how I was doing. Visiting her in this way was like joining her in a very clear dream. On the fourth day the firmness of her personality began to shift. The focus of the voice I heard in those meditations began to speak of love and acceptance. She seemed to slowly dissolve, gradually becoming light. The quality of her voice softened and widened, sounding like a lovely whisper in a giant room. I knew that she was ready and had let go of her life. The next morning I got a call that she had died. Minutes after the call from the hospital, my mother came to me, not as a physical form, but as a presence that I heard, felt, and saw with an inner awareness. She said not to worry, that she was happy and safe and that she would always love me and be connected to me and that I should take care of Bill, her husband of forty-eight years. Then she disappeared. For the next several days I could have brief conversations with her, but she was still accepting what was happening to her. Then she went away. After about a year I could speak to her again. Since then I have experienced her as a gentle light within my being.

About two months ago, while again walking on the ridge near my house, my mother came to me. She told me that it might be hard for me to contact her for a while. She was coming in to body again, and would be born in South Africa. Then she disappeared. My mother was greatly influenced by my stepfather, who had negative views on race and differences among people. I couldn't help wondering at the lessons my mother had chosen to work out. Oddly, a week or so after this incident, at a dinner with friends, one of the guests reported an almost identical story that had happened to her several weeks before.

Experiences with my clients have taught me so much. Several years ago I had a client who was a young man of twenty-one. He had not slept well in the previous year, and was barely able to work. The year before, he met and fell in love with a young woman his age. Neither of them had experienced love and intimate connection before. Both of their early lives had been filled with trauma and separation, so to find each other and to love and be loved was a profound and healing experience for both of them. They were inseparable. One day while climbing together on the rocks by the ocean in Marin County, she fell at his feet and died. He was unbearably stricken to his core.

While working with him that first day, it became obvious that he had never let her go, and as I was soon to discover, she had not let him go either. I put him on the treatment table and began an acupuncture session to balance him with the focus on helping to regain his own individuality again. As I worked on him, I soon became aware of an energy and a voice in the room beside me. I kept hearing the word, "Plaid. Plaid."

Several times the word was very clearly spoken to me.

Finally, a little unsure, I asked, "Does the word 'plaid' mean anything to you?"

"My girlfriend loved my plaid shirts," he answered, and began to cry.

I stayed with him until he relaxed and dropped into the state of reverie that often comes during an acupuncture session. Leaving him to quietly integrate, I went into my office in the next room and started making notes. Almost immediately, the energy and voice from the next room started to speak to me.

"What are you doing here? He's paying you. You should be in the next room working on him. You should be with him!"

The ephemeral voice continued to badger me for several minutes. When I finally went back to the next room, the young man was just waking up. I asked him,

"Was your girlfriend pushy?"

"Yes," he answered with an emphatic smile.

"Well, she still is," I said, chuckling.

When I told him what had happened, he laughed and said through his tears that in an unexpected way this created an opening for him to get perspective and let go a bit.

When he left that day, he asked me, "Do you talk to dead people very often?"

"No," I answered, because I had never really thought about it that way before. Later I realized I did.

The young man and I worked together for several more sessions on letting her go and having it be okay to have his own life on earth without her lingering presence, but still hold the beautiful connection with her in his heart. He realized that holding on to her was keeping her spirit from the next stage of its own journey.

As I have discussed earlier in this book, for seven years I spent a great deal of time in the country of Nepal. My main teacher was a profound Tibetan Lama named Dabsang Rinpoche.

I first saw his face in meditation in the States, and later met two Lamas in Taiwan who, after showing me his picture and hearing of my story, brought to me to meet him in Nepal. It was unbelievable luck and good fortune to be accepted as a student by him and then to spend time with him during those years. I came to love him and feel connected to him very deeply. Our connection was and is profound and transcendental on many levels. Even today, all these years later, the miracle of this fortunate connection is still revealing itself. Just when I think I understand, surprising gems keep coming to me from him.

After I returned to the United States, I kept a picture of my teacher on the dashboard of my car. One day I noticed that the picture had gotten so faded that I could barely see his face and I perceived that he was dying. Immediately I went home, called the monastery in Nepal, and found out that he was very weak and ill. Several days later I flew to Nepal, only to find that he had been taken to a hospital in Hong Kong. I stayed in Boudhanath, waiting in the monastery with the very sad monks. Two weeks later, Rinpoche returned, very weak and hardly able to speak audibly. We were able to spend some time together, and he gave me some final instructions. Then he was flown back to the hospital in Hong Kong.

My funds and schedule only allowed me to be away for a month, so I had to return home while he was still alive. A few days later I returned to California, not knowing what would happen. About a week after that, I got a call from the monastery letting me know that he had died several days before. The monk who was called Thubten told me that Rinpoche's heart had stayed warm for seven days after he died. Many nurses and doctors kept coming into his room to touch his still-warm chest. Against hospital rules, they let his body remain in the bed until his chest cooled. Even after a week his body showed no signs of odor or decay.

I felt terrible because I did not have enough money left to go back for his funeral. However, later that same day a friend called and asked if I would be willing to work for him for a few weeks. He had business in Nepal and Thailand that he knew I could easily handle, but I would have to leave immediately. I could not believe it. I was being paid to go back to Nepal!

When I arrived back in Boudhnath, Rinpoche's body had been put in a kudung, a kind of casket where the body is seated in the meditation position and packed in salt. The kudung was put in a place of honor in the monastery and a forty-nine-day ceremony was performed day and night.

Every day for the next few days I meditated by his body. During the first day, I was able to connect to and be with his awareness. Each day it seemed to expand further out into the universe. I did my best to follow him out. Finally, I could not expand out any further and had to let him go. Since then he has remained a source of help and guidance, even shifting things in the physical world. Hopefully I will have the opportunity write more about him in future books. My experience with him was one of my first communicating with a living consciousness beyond a body.

In writing this, I was surprised when I realized how many stories about death and beyond I have had. When these kinds of things happen, they do not seem strange or even unusual. When these things began to happen to me, I had not sought them out, nor had I thought about the idea of interacting with those who have passed on at all. I would guess, though, that the percentage of us who have had these experiences is very high. It is very common to hear that someone's recently departed spouse or relative has spoken to them or that they could feel their presence.

I will relate one last story about a new friend of mine, David. David is a warm, creative psychiatrist with a leaning toward the rational and scientific. As far as I know he has had no particular belief in the continuing consciousness of those who have died, but here is a story that he related to us at dinner one evening.

David's father, who had been a rather forceful and stern presence, had died. The family had all traveled to the funeral, and afterward they were at the family home having dinner. David was sitting at the head of the table. He recalls suddenly beginning to speak in his father's voice, with his father's same stern and imposing manner. His father continued to speak through him for several minutes, saying goodbye to various family members. Then he felt his body relax, and he was back to being himself again. David recounts that no one at the table acknowledged what they had witnessed. No one even mentioned what had just happened to them. After a pause, they just continued with the conversation. This fairly straight-ahead guy told the story with a openness and normalcy that, if you think about it, was in direct counterpoint to the unusualness of his story.

These experiences at the edge of death are very normal parts of our lives. Most of the time, they just seem so matter-of-fact that we do not pay much attention to them. Many of us have had them. Many more of us have had them and just did not notice or believe what had happened.

My experiences working with dying patients in hospitals and later in my private practice changed how I understood things. It is common, when working with terminal patients who are open and accepting of their death as a spiritual experience, to see a golden-white beam of light ascending from their head. Though this is not a linear process, I have used this phenomenon as an indicator of how close to their time they are. It is not until later, often much later, that it occurs to you how beautiful and "out there" these experiences really are.

When we consider death from this perspective, it does not have to be a somber affair. Why couldn't we have a jubilant ceremony for those who have transitioned, wishing them well and opening the possibility that we will continue to have them as an active part of our life, just in a very different way?

Our understanding and acceptance of death is a natural part of who we are. When we let go of our thoughts, fears, and fixations about death and drop in to our primal sense of it, death will be a comfort. It is a ticket home. It is natural that as we get older we are more accepting and understanding of it.

Animals understand death. If two dogs are very close and have spent their lives together, chasing and playing out their days, and have come to love each other in the unassuming way of dogs, it is important when one dies that the other gets to see him and sniff his body. If the remaining dog does not get to see the body of his friend, it is not uncommon for him to search for days and months, longing for his lost companion, wondering where he is hiding.

I believe this is important for humans as well. When we have a chance to be with the body of someone we have known, it is clear that the greatest part of them, the part we loved and fished with and argued with and had mysteries with, is no longer there. In those moments, if you close your eyes and feel your love for them in your heart, you can find them, connected with the momentum of your mutual affection in the pristine awareness in the timeless reality that holds us all.

Once you get past the resistance to it, death is the ultimate opportunity for spiritual awakening. In the face of death, the intrinsic value of "things" finds balance and perspective. The awareness of death also highlights the preciousness of life, as well as the irrelevance and quixotic nature of time. Like dew in the sparkling sunlight, death highlights the specialness of the little things that might be too mundane for our busy attention. When we remember what death means, it wakes us and shakes us to see the infinite specialness of each moment. No two people in the world are the same, nor is any moment in any life. Between the in breath and out breath you just took, how many moments did you miss?

How many universes collided or danced?

The miracles are endless. The endless is the miracle.

The meaning of death dissolves the meaning of time. Time is a gorgeous plaything, useful but of no lasting value. Once we can relax about death we can relax about life. Once we can relax about life, we can look beyond the boundaries of where we came from and where we might be going. In the realm of linearity we can see our life as a continuation of consciousness that holds lives and experiences that are both simple and endless. We can see ahead and behind. The infinite is close in either direction. Many lives become one life. Days in a year, years in a life, lives in a bigger life.

As the reality of this "big life" becomes familiar, we can begin to focus on what could be next. In this way we can see our life in terms of where we have gotten to and who we have become. We can create our next step and even offer who we are to whatever our deep self deems essential. If this singular life is indeed a preparation for the next, it makes sense to consider where we are and what class we might want to sign up for next.

Deep Happy Inner Practice

Facing Death

Every one of us will come to our own death one day, along with all the fears and feelings that come up when we do.

Relax and let yourself think about the possibility of your death. Pay attention to whatever fear or emotions come up. Try not to push them away. Accept them; they are normal.

Maybe you don't feel anything, and you think that you do not have any fear about it. Maybe you don't, but you probably do. Let yourself imagine your body fading away.

Do you feel fear in the body? Notice where it is. The fear is in the body, not our bigger consciousness.

Work with this gradually over a few weeks, months, or years.

Become interested in whatever your experience is. Does a part of you welcome death? Be as honest with yourself as you can be.

Is there a part of you that is not fearful or upset at the idea of death?

Ask your body how it feels about dissolving back into the earth.

Ask your spirit or inner self how it feels to return to the source. This is a very personal thing to do.

If you can, let go of any resistance.

Imagine yourself dissolving into space.

Imagine yourself being held and loved by the universe . . . forever.

Go there when you are ready.

15

Deep Happy Full Circle

Everyday Ashram

In the Indian tradition, an ashram is a place of retreat. It is a quiet and sacred place where we can go to heal and renew and find our way again. Ashrams are designed to be serene and wonderful places where the happy and deep essence of our spiritual experience is ever present. In most ashrams it is as easy to meditate and rest in stillness as it is to not do these things in the usual chaos and dizziness of the "normal" world that most of us call home. I have spent weeks and months and years in ashrams and spiritual retreats, and have always benefited from that time. However, spiritual places can also be crazy places.

Resting in stillness is not always sublime. Up from the stillness can come all that is not still and settled within us. Even as we get further down the line and seem to have little residue left inside us, the power of sacred stillness becomes a wonderful and intense magnifying glass, using the focused light of awareness to burn the last bits of any lingering unfinished business that may keep us from the infinite simplicity of being. I guess you could say that it is both the beginning and the fulfillment of everything—resting in the complete and unconstructed experience of whatever arises. This process is known as "self-liberation through direct awareness." It simply means that as we hold the awareness of any thought, sensation, experience, or phenomenal perception in complete acceptance without any kind of preconception or filtering, the thought, experience, sensation, or perception dissolves, revealing its intrinsic pristine nature. In other words, as we see and experience the innate truth of anything, the illusion of its appearances reveals itself to be empty of finite existence, and yet at the same time full of infinite possibility.

So what does that mean exactly?

It means that as we are continually able to free ourselves from the past experiences that we hold in our bodies and minds and see things as they really are, on all levels, we may find that the essence of everything, of all things, is the essence of us.

How can I get there if I cannot possibly take the time off or spend the money to have my own ashram experience?

In the first place, the most important thing to remember is that there is nothing to get and no place to go. The presence of the infinite and sacred is as much a part of us as our skin or bones. It fills the space between everything, and since everything is ultimately space, that means that our essence is in the moment beyond imagining, and that the only real ashram is our awareness.

Although taking sacred time and space for ourselves is a precious thing, with care and intention we can re-create our life and adjust our selves so that each moment can hold the fragrance of sacred space. This is the real purpose of Deep Happy.

The outer disturbances of life can be fully experienced and dealt with while at the same time rarely if ever affecting our pristine inner resonance and our connection to the primal field that connects all things. When the events of our life and our world are experienced this way, any resistance we have or any instance of being pulled from our centered awareness or even any misperception can be recognized for what it is, and eventually just dissolves. Even when it seems we are pulled into the chaos of aggression and reaction, there is still part of us that is untouched, watching with humor as the game of outer reactivity plays itself out. Very often in the world it is important to express will or a concerned and passionate response. I don't believe that we should hide from the energized parts of our personality—they are also the part of consciousness through biology. The more we are healed and the clearer our enlightened purpose, the less we have to be concerned about. Once the instrument is properly tuned, then whatever is played on it is also in tune. Life and the expression of it through energy and will are huge gifts. When our hearts are clear and settled, the last bits of judgment of our own self-expression are released and we can trust our passion and fire because it is the unhindered creative extension of our pristine nature.

I'll say it once more. Each moment is sacred. Each thing or action, no matter how seemingly profane it might appear, dissolves in its own intrinsic essence as space and light. The bandwidth between the sacred and impure is the illusion of separation itself. As we become used to simultaneously holding and living within both, the richness and depth of life's experiences deepen us without clouding over the vastness and simplicity of our essential being.

Deep Happy.

About the Author

PETER FAIRFIELD LAc, is a teacher, healer and acupuncturist who spent many years with Tibetan yogis, Taoists adepts, Qigong masters and physicians from Tibet, Nepal, China, Thailand, Taiwan, and the U.S. He has researched Asian medical and spiritual systems and their relationship to modern scientific, psychological, and biomedical paradigms for over 40 years. He lectures nationally on the clinical and practical applications of these systems. In his practice he uses his intuitive awareness and other modalities for physical, emotional and spiritual development, as well as teaches Qigong and meditation to connect to DEEP HAPPY. He practices in Mill Valley, California with his wife Conde. An avid hiker and traveler, he plays and collects guitars and teaches healing and transformative processes internationally. Visit Peter at *www.deephappylife.com.*

To Our Readers

Weiser Books, an imprint of Red Wheel/Weiser, publishes books across the entire spectrum of occult, esoteric, speculative, and New Age subjects. Our mission is to publish quality books that will make a difference in people's lives without advocating any one particular path or field of study. We value the integrity, originality, and depth of knowledge of our authors.

Our readers are our most important resource, and we appreciate your input, suggestions, and ideas about what you would like to see published.

Visit our website *www.redwheelweiser.com,* where you can learn about our upcoming books and free downloads, and be sure to go to *www.redwheelweiser.com/newsletter/* to sign up for newsletters and exclusive offers.

You can also contact us at *info@redwheelweiser.com* or at:

Red Wheel/Weiser, LLC
665 Third Street, Suite 400
San Francisco, CA 94107